MICROWAVE RECIPES FOR ONE OR TWO

Margaret Weale

ANGELL EDITIONS

Newton Abbot, Devon

Contents

Cover: Boeuf bourguignonne (page 30); Baked jacket potato (page 40) with yoghurt and chive dressing; Raspberry delight (page 53) — on Micratex Black Orchid

Chicken curry (page 33); Brown rice (page 42) — on Micratex Jazz

Introduction

Cooking for one or two

A well-balanced, varied diet is essential for good health, and sensible meal planning is just as important when cooking for only one or two as it is when cooking for a family. Everyday food can provide all the nutrients essential to help our bodies function correctly and also follow the current trend towards healthier eating.

Cooking small quantities of food for one or two people in the conventional way can take just as long as cooking larger quantities for a family and create just as much washing-up too. Indeed it can often seem more trouble than it is worth and we may be tempted not to bother, even though we know that a cooked meal is a better, healthier choice than eating cakes and biscuits to satisfy our hunger.

With a microwave oven, smaller quantities of food take less time to cook than larger quantities. Tasty, wholesome meals and snacks can be produced so quickly and easily that cooking becomes a pleasure rather than a dreaded chore. Washing-up is reduced to a minimum too, since food can so often be cooked and served in the same dish or on the same plate. When separate serving plates are needed, these can be heated by placing them under the cooking dish in the oven. A microwave oven is much cheaper to run that a conventional cooker because it cooks food so quickly, and of course there is no need to pre-heat the oven before use.

Most microwave oven recipes, like conventional recipes, cater for four to six, rather than one or two people. Unlike conventional recipes, however, they cannot be so easily converted to serve a smaller number. When the quantity of food is decreased in microwave oven recipes, the cooking time must be reduced, and correct timing is essential for acceptable results.

In this book you will find a wide variety of recipes, using fresh and frozen ingredients, which cater for one or two. These recipes have been chosen after having discussions with many people of all ages, who live in small households of one or two people, to find out what foods they genuinely wanted to defrost, reheat or cook in their microwave oven. The seven day menus provide ideas for a healthy eating pattern and, of course, the midday and evening meals can easily be interchanged to suit your lifestyle.

The manufacturer's handbook supplied with your particular oven will have provided essential information related to the theory and principles of microwave cookery. However, you may feel the need for further guidelines and tips on the basic techniques, to help you learn the general do's and don'ts of microwave cookery and these can be found in 'Beginning Microwave Cookery' by the same author published by Angell Editions in paperback at £3.95.

Selecting cooking containers

When selecting cooking containers, remember that metal pots and pans must never be used in a microwave oven. China or pottery with a metallic trim or manufacturer's mark in gold or silver on the base are also unsuitable. The size of the container should match the amount of food; but foods with lots of liquid, such as rice and pasta, will tend to bubble up during cooking, so it is essential to use containers which are large enough to prevent spillage.

Remove foil wrappings from food before placing it in the oven and replace metal twist-ties on roasting bags with string or elastic bands. Never place a can of food in the oven, always turn the contents into an ovenproof container. Provided your manufacturer's instructions allow, you can use small, smooth pieces of aluminium foil to shield the narrower ends of meat, fish or poultry, to prevent overcooking. Foil must never touch any part of the oven interior.

Specially designed microwave cookware, browning dishes, roasting racks and thermometers are readily available and should be used according to the manufacturer's instructions.

Power output levels used in this book

Most microwave ovens now have at least two power output levels. HIGH or FULL POWER setting is used to cook most foods quickly. LOW or DEFROST setting is used not only to defrost frozen foods but also to cook certain foods which benefit from longer, slower cooking, such as meat casseroles and baked egg custard. These are the two settings which are used throughout this book and they are based on ovens with a maximum output of approximately 650W–700W on HIGH or FULL POWER and a lower output of approximately 200W–260W on LOW or DEFROST setting. For ovens with lower outputs, times will have to be increased slightly. Times given throughout this book should be used as a guide only, since ovens, even with the same output, vary in efficiency. The golden rule is to undercook rather than risk overcooking food. Undercooked food can always be returned to the microwave oven for further cooking, but there is no remedy for overcooked, spoiled food.

Measuring ingredients

The recipes in this book have been tested using both metric and imperial measures. It is important to weigh and measure accurately. The exact metric equivalent of an imperial 1oz is 28.35g, but the accepted equivalent is 25g. This means that the total volume of cooked food can vary slightly, depending on whether imperial or metric measurements are used. For this reason it is essential to follow either all imperial or all metric measurements, never mix the two. All spoon measures are level unless otherwise stated.

Measuring spoon sizes

Standard spoon measurements are used in the recipes.
1 tablespoon = 1 × 15ml spoon
1 teaspoon   = 1 × 5ml spoon
½ teaspoon   = 2.5ml
all spoon measures are level unless otherwise stated.

Weight

Imperial	Accepted Metric Equivalent	Exact Metric Equivalent
1oz	25g	28.35g
2oz	50g	56.7g
3oz	75g	85.05g
4oz	100g	113.4g
5oz	125g	141.75g
6oz	150g	170.1g
7oz	175g	198.45g
8oz	225g	226.8g
9oz	250g	255.15g
10oz	275g	283.5g
11oz	300g	311.85g
12oz	350g	340.2g
13oz	375g	368.54g
14oz	400g	396.9g
15oz	425g	425.24g
16oz (1lb)	450g	453.6g

Volume

Imperial	Accepted Metric Equivalent	Exact Metric Equivalent
1fl oz	30ml	28.41ml
¼pt	150ml	142.06ml
½pt	300ml	284.12ml
¾pt	450ml	426.19ml
1pt	600ml	568.25ml

Length

Imperial	Metric Equivalent
½in	1.25cm
1in	2.5cm
6in	15cm
7in	17.5cm
8in	20cm
9in	22.5cm
10in	25cm

Beverages and snacks

Instant tea *(serves 1)*

1 teabag
180ml (6fl oz) cold water
sugar, milk or lemon to taste

1 Place teabag in a cup.
2 Pour in the water and microwave on HIGH for
   1¾ min or until just boiling.
3 Remove teabag and add sugar, milk or lemon
   to taste.

Note:
2 cups will require approx 3¼ min. Larger quantities are best made conventionally.

Instant coffee *(serves 1)*

180ml (6fl oz) cold water
1 teaspoon instant coffee
sugar, milk or cream to taste

1 Measure water into a cup or mug.
2 Microwave on HIGH for 1¾ min or until just
   boiling.
3 Stir in coffee and add sugar, milk or cream to
   taste.

Note:
1 *2 cups will require approx 3¼ min. Larger
   quantities are best made conventionally.*
2 *If preferred use milk instead of water. Heat 1
   cup of milk for approx 1½ min and 2 cups of
   milk for approx 2½ min, to prevent boiling
   and spillage.*

Instant gaelic coffee *(serves 1)*

180ml (6fl oz) water
1 teaspoon instant coffee
1 teaspoon demerara sugar
2 tablespoons whisky
1 tablespoon whipping cream

1 Pour the water into an Irish coffee goblet or
   serving glass (not lead crystal) and microwave on HIGH for 1½ min.

2 Stir in the coffee and sugar, stirring until dissolved. Add whisky.
3 Microwave on HIGH for a further 30 sec.
4 Carefully pour the cream over the back of a
   warm spoon to float on top of the coffee. If
   preferred, the cream can be whipped and
   spooned on top.

Hot chocolate *(serves 1)*

180ml (6fl oz) milk, or milk and water
3 teaspoons drinking chocolate powder, or as
   directed on pack
sugar to taste
whipped cream

1 Measure the milk, or milk and water, into a
   cup without metal trim and microwave on
   HIGH for 1½ min, until hot but not boiling.
2 Stir in the chocolate powder. Add sugar to
   taste and top with whipped cream.

VARIATIONS
Hot chocolate de luxe: proceed as above omitting the cream. After step 2 float a marshmallow
on top of the hot chocolate and heat on HIGH
for a further 10–15 sec, during which time the
marshmallow will puff up and soften. The
marshmallow will slowly collapse when removed from the oven.
Hot chocolate with rum: stir in 1 tablespoon of
rum at step 2 above.

Hot cocoa *(serves 1)*

1 teaspoon cocoa, or as directed on pack
sugar to taste
180ml (6fl oz) milk, or milk and water

1 Blend the cocoa and sugar with a little of the
   measured milk, or milk and water, in a cup.
2 Stir in remaining liquid and microwave on
   HIGH for 1½ min until steaming but not boiling.
3 Stir before serving.

VARIATION
Hot mocha: add ¼ teaspoon coffee granules with
the cocoa. Proceed as above. Serve topped with
whipped cream.

*Breakfast grapefruit (page 16); Whole kipper for one
(page 20); Compôte of dried fruit (page 54) – on
Adams Sharon*

To cook bacon (serves 1)

2 rashers bacon

1 Snip the bacon rind and fat at regular intervals to prevent it curling during cooking.
2 Place the rashers on double thickness kitchen paper on a plate without metal trim. Cover lightly with kitchen paper to prevent splattering.
3 Microwave on HIGH for 2–2½ min or until cooked as preferred. Do not overcook or bacon will become brittle.
4 Remove paper immediately, to prevent sticking.

Note:
1 *When cooking larger quantities of bacon, overlap the fat with the lean, or place the rashers in a suitable shallow dish or on a microwave roasting rack in a dish to catch the fat. Cover lightly with kitchen paper and cook on HIGH allowing 4–4½ min for 4 rashers. Rearrange the bacon rashers during the cooking period.*
2 *Cooking times may vary according to type, thickness and cure of bacon.*
3 *Bacon can also be cooked in a microwave browning dish.*

VARIATION
Toasted bacon sandwich: toast bread conventionally. Brush one side of the toasted bread with bacon fat before making the sandwich. If necessary, reheat the sandwich on a piece of kitchen paper, or white napkin, on a serving plate, for about 30 sec on HIGH.

Browning dish breakfast for two

2 eggs, at room temperature
4 rashers bacon
2 medium tomatoes, halved

1 Break the eggs onto saucers and pierce the yolks carefully with the tines of a fork. Snip the bacon fat at regular intervals to prevent curling during cooking.
2 Preheat a microwave browning dish according to manufacturer's instructions. Grease only if recommended.
3 Immediately place the bacon and tomatoes around the outside of the dish, pressing them down onto the hot surface.
4 Microwave on HIGH for 2 min.
5 Turn the bacon and tomatoes over and slide the eggs into the dish. Baste the eggs with bacon fat.
6 Cover the dish with its lid and continue cooking on HIGH for about 2 min, until eggs are set.
7 Leave to stand, covered, for 2 min to finish cooking, before serving.

Bacon and egg on a plate (serves 1)

2 rashers bacon
1 egg, at room temperature

1 Snip the bacon fat at regular intervals to prevent curling during cooking.
2 Arrange bacon rashers around the outside of a plate.
3 Cover with kitchen paper and microwave on HIGH for 1½ min or until almost cooked. Turn bacon over.
4 Break the egg into a buttered ramekin or small individual dish. Pierce the yolk carefully with a fork and cover.
5 Place the dish in the centre of the plate with the bacon.
6 Microwave on HIGH for 45–60 sec depending on size of egg used and storage temperature.
7 Leave to stand for 2 min to finish cooking, before serving.

VARIATION
Bacon, egg and tomato on a plate: follow steps 1 to 5 above, omitting step 3. Do not cover egg dish at step 4. Cut a tomato in half and place on plate with bacon and egg dish. Cover with kitchen paper and microwave on HIGH for 2 min or until cooked as preferred. Leave to stand for 1–2 min to finish cooking, before serving.

Cheesy baked beans on toast (serves 1)

1 × 150g (5.3oz) can baked beans
1 thick slice of bread, toasted and buttered if
  preferred
dash of Worcestershire sauce
1 slice of processed or Cheddar cheese
paprika

1 Place beans in a small ovenproof bowl.
2 Cover and microwave on HIGH for 1 min.
3 Place the toast on a serving plate, and top
  with the beans. Sprinkle with Worcestershire
  sauce.
4 Top with the cheese and microwave on HIGH
  for 30 sec, or until the cheese has started to
  melt.
5 Stand for 1 min before serving, sprinkled
  with paprika.

Note: *To reduce washing up, beans may be
placed on the toast before heating. Cover
loosely with a small piece of greaseproof paper
and microwave on* HIGH *for 1½ min. Top with
cheese and continue heating on* HIGH *for a
further 30 sec or until cheese starts to melt.*

VARIATION
Substitute 1 small can of spaghetti or ravioli for
the baked beans.

Ham, egg and cheese baps (serves 1–2)

2 eggs
2 tablespoons milk
salt and pepper
1 slice boiled ham, cut into small pieces
2 wholemeal or cheese baps
cheese slices to cover baps

1 Beat the eggs and milk together in an ovenproof bowl. Add seasoning.
2 Cook on HIGH for 1 min. Stir the cooked egg
  mixture from the edges into the centre and
  stir in the ham.
3 Cook on HIGH for a further 30 sec or until
  eggs are almost cooked. Set aside and leave to
  stand, covered.
4 Cut the baps in half and arrange on a plate.

5 Lay a slice of cheese on the bottom halves and
  microwave all four halves on HIGH for 1 min.
6 Spoon the scrambled egg mixture onto the
  cheese and top with the remaining halves.
  Serve at once.

Browning dish cheese sandwich (serves 2)

4 sandwich slices processed cheese, plain or
  with onion
4 slices bread
butter

1 Preheat microwave browning dish according
  to manufacturer's instructions.
2 Meanwhile place 2 slices of cheese between
  each 2 slices of bread, and butter the outside
  of the sandwiches on both sides.
3 Using oven gloves, remove the dish from the
  oven and place on a protected work surface.
4 Place the sandwiches immediately on the base
  of the preheated dish and flatten them with a
  palette knife to ensure overall contact with
  the hot base.
5 Leave the sandwiches for 20–30 sec or until
  brown underneath.
6 Turn over, preferably onto another unused
  part of the heated base. Press down as before
  and leave for a further 30–45 sec to brown
  the second side.
7 If necessary, return the sandwiches in the dish
  to the oven and microwave on HIGH for
  15–30 sec to finish melting the cheese.

Note:
1 *The browning dish gets very hot. Use
  ovengloves.*
2 *Work surfaces must be protected from the
  heat of the browning dish.*
3 *The sandwiches are browned in the dish
  outside the oven.*

VARIATIONS
1 Spread pickle, mustard or ketchup between
  the cheese slices.
2 Fill sandwiches with 1 thin slice of ham and 1
  slice of cheese.
3 Use unprocessed cheese, cut into thin slices.

Welsh rarebit (serves 1–2)

100g (4oz) strong cheese, grated
½ teaspoon dry mustard powder
pepper
dash of Worcestershire sauce
2 tablespoons brown ale or milk
2 thick slices of bread, toasted conventionally
sliced tomato
cress or watercress to garnish

1 Place cheese, mustard, pepper, Worcestershire sauce and ale or milk in an ovenproof bowl.
2 Microwave on HIGH for 30 sec. Stir well and microwave on HIGH for a further 15–30 sec or until cheese has melted.
3 Stir well and spread over toast.
4 Brown under a preheated grill before serving topped with sliced tomato and garnished with cress or watercress.

VARIATION
Muffin rarebit: replace toasted bread with split toasted muffins, preferably wholemeal or cheese.

Mushrooms on toast (serves 1)

25g (1oz) butter
100g (4oz) mushrooms, sliced
15g (½oz) plain flour
150ml (¼pt) milk
salt and pepper
2 slices wholemeal bread, toasted

1 Place the butter in a Pyrex measuring jug and melt on HIGH for about 45 sec.
2 Stir in mushrooms and cook on HIGH for 1 min.
3 Stir in flour, blend in milk and cook on HIGH for 2½–3 min, stirring every minute.
4 Season to taste and serve on toast.

VARIATION
Cheesy mushrooms on toast: at the end of step 3 stir in 25g (1oz) grated mature Cheddar or crumbled blue cheese.

10

Pitta steaklet (serves 1)

1 × 85g (3oz) frozen steaklet
tomato, barbecue or sweetcorn relish
1 wholemeal or plain pitta bread
shredded iceberg lettuce or Chinese leaves
a little chopped onion, or spring onion
sliced radish and/or cucumber
1 tomato, sliced or chopped
salt and pepper

1 Place the steaklet on an ovenproof plate and cover loosely with kitchen paper.
2 Microwave on HIGH for 1½ min then turn steaklet over.
3 Spread relish on steaklet and cook on HIGH for a further 1 min or until cooked.
4 Slit the pitta bread to form a pouch.
5 Place the steaklet in the pouch and fill with the salad ingredients.
6 Sprinkle filling with seasoning and serve immediately.

Note: *The pitta bread can be placed on kitchen paper and warmed in the microwave oven on* LOW *for 8–10 sec after step 3. This makes it easier to slit than when cold. Do not overheat or the bread will toughen.*

Sardines and tomato on toast (serves 1)

1 × 120g (4½oz) can sardines, drained
lemon juice
2 slices bread, toasted conventionally and buttered if preferred
1 tomato, skinned and sliced

1 If preferred, the sardines may first be boned before mashing with a little lemon juice.
2 Place the toast on a serving plate, without metal trim, and arrange or spread the sardines on it.
3 Top with tomato slices and microwave on HIGH for 1½ min.

Note: *For 2 servings, double the above quantities and microwave on* HIGH *for about 2½ min.*

Soup in a cup (page 62); Pitta Steaklet (above); Muffin rarebit (above) – on Micratex Spring Garden

Crumpet pizzas (serves 1)

2 rashers streaky bacon
2 crumpets, plain or wholemeal
2 medium tomatoes, thinly sliced
pizza seasoning or dried mixed herbs
2 slices processed cheese
2 olives

1 Snip the bacon at regular intervals and place the rashers on kitchen paper on a plate.
2 Cover with kitchen paper and cook on HIGH for 1 min or until cooked, time taken depending on thickness of bacon.
3 Remove paper from bacon to prevent sticking.
4 Arrange the tomato on the crumpets and sprinkle with seasoning or herbs. Using scissors snip the bacon into small pieces and place on top of tomato.
5 Cut the cheese slices into strips and lay these in a criss-cross pattern over each crumpet. Top with olives.
6 Place the crumpets on a serving plate and microwave on HIGH for 1 min or until cheese has melted.
7 Serve immediately.

VARIATIONS
1 Instead of bacon place a slice of salami on each crumpet before topping with tomato and cheese.
2 Use a split wholemeal, plain or cheese muffin instead of 2 crumpets.
3 Canned tomatoes can be used for this recipe.

Pie and mushy peas (serves 1)

1 ready-cooked individual meat pie, at room temperature, weighing 125–150g (5–6oz)
1 × 290g (10½oz) can mushy peas

1 Remove foil container and place the pie preferably on a microwave roasting rack or on kitchen paper on an ovenproof serving plate, without metal trim.
2 Cover loosely with kitchen paper.

3 Microwave on HIGH for 1½ min. Leave to stand.
4 Meanwhile empty half the contents of the can of peas into a small ovenproof bowl. Reserve remainder for future use.
5 Cover the bowl and heat the peas on HIGH for about 1 min.
6 Remove the kitchen paper from the pie and spoon the peas over the pie.

Note: *As a main course rather than a snack, serve with a jacket potato which can be cooked first and wrapped in foil, shiny side in, to keep warm while heating the pie and peas.*

Hot dogs (serves 2)

1 medium onion, peeled and chopped
1 tablespoon water
4 soft finger rolls
4 frankfurter sausages
tomato or other relish

1 Place the onion and water in an ovenproof bowl.
2 Cover and microwave on HIGH for 3 min, stirring or shaking after 1½ min. Drain cooked onion.
3 Split the rolls in half lengthways and place a frankfurter and cooked onion in each.
4 Arrange hot dogs on kitchen paper on a plate.
5 Cover with kitchen paper and microwave on HIGH for 2 min, rearranging the hot dogs after 1 min.
6 Serve topped with favourite relish.

Note:
1 *1 hot dog will only need heating for about 40 sec on HIGH; 2 hot dogs will require about 1 min.*
2 *The hot dogs can be individually wrapped, ready to serve, in paper napkins. Use only white, not coloured, napkins to prevent transfer of colour.*
3 *Any leftover frankfurters can be used in the recipe for Main Course Frankfurter and Bean Soup (page 14).*

Burger in a bun *(serves 2)*

2 × 100g (4oz) frozen burgers or quarter
   pounders
2 hamburger buns or baps
mustard or burger relish
pickled dill cucumber, sliced

1 Place the burgers, apart, either on a microwave roasting rack or ovenproof plate and
defrost on LOW for 3 min. Stand for 5 min.
2 Cook on HIGH for 4–5 min or until no longer
pink in the centre. Turn burgers over after 2
min.
3 Leave to stand for 2 min.
4 Place in split buns and spread with relish.
5 Arrange the pickled dill cucumber on the
burgers and replace the tops of the buns.

Note:
1 *For one serving, proceed as above, halving
the ingredients. Defrost the burger on* LOW
for 2 min; then cook on HIGH *for 2½–3½ min,
turning it over after 1½ min.*
2 *To give colour, burgers can be brushed over
with equal parts Worcestershire or soy sauce
and water. Alternatively they can be cooked
on a microwave browning dish.*

VARIATION
Cheeseburger in a bun *(serves 1 or 2)*: defrost
and cook 1 or 2 burgers as given above and
place in split hamburger buns. Top each burger
with a slice of cheese. Place the filled buns on
absorbent kitchen paper on a plate and microwave on HIGH, allowing about 30–45 sec for 1
cheeseburger and about 45–60 sec for 2
cheeseburgers, or until cheese just starts to melt.
Do not overheat.

Roes on toast *(serves 1–2)*

100–150g (4–6oz) soft herring roes
25g (1oz) butter or margarine
lemon juice
1–2 slices bread
salt and pepper
lemon wedges
chopped parsley

1 Wash the roes and dry thoroughly on kitchen
paper.
2 Place the butter or margarine in a shallow
ovenproof dish and microwave on HIGH for 1
min.
3 Add the roe and coat them in the melted
butter. Sprinkle with lemon juice.
4 Cover and microwave on LOW for 2 min.
5 Turn roes over, re-cover and cook on LOW for
a further 2–2½ min or until cooked.
6 Leave to stand, covered, while toasting the
bread.
7 Season the roes to taste and serve on the toast
accompanied by lemon wedges and sprinkled
with chopped parsley.

Soups, starters and sauces

Thick vegetable broth with rice
(serves 2 generously)

1 small onion, peeled and thinly sliced
1 stick celery, thinly sliced
2 tablespoons chopped green or red pepper
2 teaspoons vegetable oil
1×225g (7.9oz) can baked beans in tomato
  sauce
1×227g (8oz) can tomatoes, roughly chopped,
  retaining juices
25g (1oz) long-grain rice
1 small courgette, thinly sliced
½ vegetable stock cube dissolved in 240ml (8fl
  oz) boiling water
salt and pepper
1 tablespoon chopped parsley

1 Place onion, celery, pepper and oil in a bowl
  or casserole.
2 Cover and microwave on HIGH for 4 min,
  stirring after 2 min.
3 Stir in remaining ingredients, mixing all well
  together.
4 Re-cover and microwave on HIGH for 45 min.
5 Stand for 5 min before serving as a filling
  lunch or supper dish.

Mushroom soup *(serves 2)*

225g (8oz) mushrooms, chopped
25g (1oz) butter
25g (1oz) plain flour
150ml (¼pt) milk
300ml (½pt) boiling chicken stock
salt and pepper

1 Place mushrooms and butter in a bowl or
  casserole.
2 Cover and microwave on HIGH for 3 min.
3 Stir in flour and gradually blend in milk and
  stock.
4 Cover and microwave on HIGH for 4 min or
  until boiling.
5 Press through a sieve, or purée in a blender or
  food processor. Season to taste.

Simple green pea soup *(serves 1)*

150g (6oz) frozen peas
4 lettuce leaves, finely shredded
good pinch of dried mint
240ml (8fl oz) almost boiling water
½ ham stock cube
salt and pepper
1 tablespoon cream or natural unsweetened
  yoghurt

1 Place the peas, lettuce leaves and mint, in an
  ovenproof bowl or casserole.
2 Cover and cook on HIGH for 3 min or until
  peas are tender.
3 Purée in a blender with the water and crumbled stock cube.
5 Reheat on HIGH for about 1 min.
6 Swirl in the cream or yoghurt before serving.

Main course frankfurter and bean soup
(serves 1–2)

15g (½oz) butter
1 medium onion, peeled and finely sliced
1 medium carrot, scraped and thinly sliced
1 scant tablespoon plain flour
300ml (½pt) hot chicken stock
50g (2oz) frozen peas
1×223g (7.9oz) can butter beans
4 canned frankfurter sausages, each cut into 4
salt and pepper

1 Place the butter, onion and carrot in a bowl
  or casserole.
2 Cover and cook on HIGH for 4 min, stirring
  after 2 min.
3 Stir in flour and gradually blend in the hot
  stock.
4 Re-cover and cook on HIGH for 3 min or until
  boiling. Stir every min.
5 Stir in the peas, butter beans and frankfurters.
6 Re-cover and cook on HIGH for 5 min. Check
  seasoning.
7 Stand, covered, for 3 min before serving with
  crusty wholemeal or French bread.

Note: *Any leftover frankfurters can be used in
the recipe for Hot Dogs (page 12).*

*Main course frankfurter and bean soup (above);
Stuffed tomatoes for two (page 17) – on Micratex
Morello*

Lentil and bacon soup *(serves 2)*

50g (2oz) red lentils
1 small onion, peeled and finely chopped
50g (2oz) lean bacon, de-rinded and finely
   chopped
450ml ($\frac{3}{4}$pt) ham stock made with 1 ham stock
   cube and boiling water
pepper
chopped parsley to garnish

1 Wash the lentils and soak for at least 2 hours.
   Drain.
2 Place the onion and bacon in a bowl or casserole.
3 Cover and microwave on HIGH for 2 min,
   stirring after 1 min.
4 Stir in the boiling stock, pepper and lentils.
5 Cover and microwave on HIGH for 15 min or
   until lentils are soft.
6 Serve sprinkled with chopped parsley, or
   purée in an electric blender or food processor
   if a smooth soup is preferred.

VARIATION
Omit uncooked bacon, cook onion with 2 teaspoons water for 1 min. Stir in 50g (2oz) chopped
cooked ham or leftover cooked bacon joint for
the final 5 min cooking time.

Meat gravy *(makes 150ml/$\frac{1}{4}$pt)*

1 teaspoon cornflour
strained meat juices
hot stock made with hot water and stock
   powder or cube
salt and pepper
gravy browning

1 Blend cornflour with a little of the strained
   meat juices in a Pyrex jug.
2 Blend in enough hot stock to make up to
   150ml ($\frac{1}{4}$pt)
3 Microwave on HIGH for 1$\frac{1}{2}$ min or until gravy
   has boiled. Stir twice during this time.
4 Season to taste and stir in a little gravy
   browning, before serving.

Croûtons *(serves 2–3)*

25g (1oz) butter
1 thick slice of brown or white bread

1 Remove the crusts from the bread and cut
   into 1.25cm ($\frac{1}{2}$in) cubes.
2 Place the butter in a shallow dish and microwave on HIGH for 30–45 sec or until melted.
3 Toss the cubes in the melted butter and cook
   on HIGH for 1 min.
4 Stir and cook on HIGH for a further 1 min.
5 Drain on kitchen paper.
6 Serve with all types of soup. Try them sprinkled over salad.

Note: *Store leftover croûtons in an airtight container. Can also be frozen.*

VARIATIONS
Herb croûtons: mix $\frac{1}{2}$ teaspoon fresh, or a pinch
of dried, herbs with the melted butter and pro-
ceed as above.
Parmesan croûtons: toss the drained croûtons in
grated Parmesan cheese.
Slimmers' croûtons: omit butter. Heat the bread
cubes on HIGH for 1 min. Stir and heat for a
further 1 min or until bread is dry.

Baked spiced grapefruit *(serves 2)*

1 grapefruit
2 teaspoons sherry
2 teaspoons dark soft brown or demerara sugar
ground cinnamon or mixed spice
1 maraschino or glacé cherry, halved

1 Cut the grapefruit in half and remove pips.
   Loosen the segments, using a sharp knife.
2 Place in individual dishes and sprinkle with
   sherry, sugar and a little cinnamon or mixed
   spice.
3 Leave to stand for about half an hour.
4 Microwave on HIGH for 1$\frac{1}{2}$–2 min, depending
   on size.
5 Serve topped with half a cherry.

VARIATION
Breakfast grapefruit: omit sherry and spice.
Sprinkle with sugar if required. Microwave on
HIGH for 1–1$\frac{1}{2}$ min and top each half grapefruit
with half a cherry before serving.

Stuffed tomatoes *(serves 2)*

1 × 198g (7oz) pack cook-in-bag frozen buttered smoked haddock
4 medium tomatoes
25g (1oz) breadcrumbs
1 tablespoon finely chopped onion or chives
1 tablespoon chopped parsley
salt and pepper

1 Make a 2.5cm (1in) slit in the top of the bag of fish and place on a plate.
2 Microwave on HIGH for 5 min and leave to stand for 2 min.
3 Meanwhile cut the tops off the tomatoes and put them on one side.
4 Carefully scoop the flesh out of the tomatoes and mix this with the breadcrumbs, onion or chives, and parsley.
5 Skin and flake the cooked haddock and stir into the tomato mixture. Season to taste.
6 Spoon the fish mixture into the tomato shells, replace tops, and place them in a circle in a shallow ovenproof dish or on an ovenproof plate.
7 Cover and microwave on HIGH for 2½ min or until heated through.
8 Serve hot or cold garnished with watercress or cress as a starter. Alternatively serve with salad as a light lunch or supper dish.

Mackerel pâté *(serves 2–4)*

1 × 170g (6oz) pack frozen kippered mackerel fillets
1 × 113g (4oz) carton curd cheese
2 teaspoons lemon juice
dash of anchovy essence
cress to garnish
lemon slices or wedges

1 Make a 2.5cm (1in) slit in the top of the bag of fillets and place it on an ovenproof plate.
2 Microwave on HIGH for 4½ min. Shake bag, leave to stand for 2 min.
3 Remove skin from fish and flake the flesh in a bowl.
4 Add cheese, lemon juice and essence.

5 For a coarse pâté, mash well with a fork. For a smooth pâté, use an electric blender or food processor, or press through a sieve.
6 Turn mixture into individual serving dishes and refrigerate.
7 Garnish with cress and serve with lemon slices or wedges, accompanied by Melba toast or freshly toasted white or wholemeal bread.

VARIATION

Kipper or smoked haddock pâté: use a pack of frozen kipper fillets or smoked haddock fillets instead of mackerel, and proceed as above.

One-stage basic white sauce
(makes 150ml/¼pt)

15g (½oz) soft margarine
15g (½oz) plain flour
150ml (¼pt) milk
salt and pepper

1 Whisk margarine, flour, milk and seasoning together in a 1 litre (1¾pt) Pyrex measuring jug.
2 Microwave on HIGH for 2½ min or until sauce has boiled and thickened. Whisk every minute.

Note: *To make 300ml (½pt) sauce, double the recipe ingredients and proceed as above, extending the cooking time to 3½ min or until sauce has boiled and thickened.*

VARIATIONS

Cheese sauce: stir in 50g (2oz) grated cheese, a pinch of cayenne pepper and a little made mustard to the thickened sauce. Cook on HIGH for a further 30 sec.
Parsley sauce: stir in 2 tablespoons chopped parsley to the thickened sauce.
Mushroom sauce: stir in 50g (2oz) finely chopped mushrooms for the final 1 min of cooking period.
Quick tomato sauce: stir in 1 tablespoon tomato purée, adding a pinch of sugar and a pinch of dried thyme or basil.

Bread sauce *(makes 300ml/½pt)*

1 small onion, peeled
2 cloves
1 bayleaf
3 peppercorns
300ml (½pt) milk
50g (2oz) breadcrumbs
15g (½oz) butter
salt and pepper

1 Stick cloves in onion and place with bayleaf, peppercorns and milk in a Pyrex jug.
2 Microwave on HIGH for 3 min. Leave to stand, covered, for at least 10 min to infuse. Uncover.
3 Stir in the breadcrumbs and butter and cook on HIGH for 4 min.
4 Remove the onion, cloves, bayleaf and peppercorns and beat well. Season to taste.
5 Beat in an extra 15g (½oz) butter.
6 Serve with chicken or turkey.

Egg custard sauce *(makes 300ml/½pt)*

300ml (½pt) milk
2 egg yolks
25g (1oz) caster sugar
few drops vanilla essence

1 Place milk in a Pyrex jug and heat on HIGH for 2 min.
2 Beat the egg yolks and sugar together in a bowl.
3 Strain the heated milk and stir into the egg and sugar mixture.
4 Stir in vanilla essence and microwave the sauce uncovered on LOW for 4 min or until creamy. Do not allow sauce to boil, or it will curdle.
5 Serve hot or cold, as a pouring sauce with baked or steamed puddings or fruit.

Note: *If a slightly thicker sauce is preferred, blend 15g (½oz) cornflour with the milk before heating. For a less rich sauce use one whole egg instead of two egg yolks.*

Custard sauce *(makes 300ml/½pt)*

1 tablespoon custard powder
1 tablespoon sugar
300ml (½pt) milk

1 Blend custard powder and sugar with a little of the measured milk, in a Pyrex or suitable jug.
2 Gradually stir in the remaining milk.
3 Microwave on HIGH for 3½ min or until sauce has boiled and thickened. Stir every minute.

Butterstotch nut sauce *(makes about 150ml/¼pt)*

50g (2oz) butter
4 tablespoons soft brown sugar
2 tablespoons golden syrup
1 tablespoon chopped nuts
squeeze of lemon juice

1 Place butter, sugar and syrup in a Pyrex jug and microwave on HIGH for 45 sec.
2 Stir well and microwave on HIGH for a further 45 sec.
3 Stir well until sugar has completely dissolved.
4 Microwave on HIGH for a further 1½ min, or until sauce has thickened, stirring every minute.
5 Stir in nuts and lemon juice.
6 Serve hot over ice-cream or baked apples.

Chocolate sauce *(makes 300ml/½pt)*

1 tablespoon cocoa, sieved
2 teaspoons cornflour
300ml (½pt) milk
25g (1oz) caster sugar or soft brown sugar
knob of butter

1 Place sieved cocoa and cornflour in a Pyrex jug of at least 600ml (1pt) capacity.
2 Blend to a smooth paste with a little of the measured milk.
3 Blend in remaining milk. Stir in sugar.
4 Microwave on HIGH for 3½ min or until sauce has boiled and thickened. Stir every minute.
5 Stir in butter.
6 Serve hot with baked or steamed puddings.

Soused herrings (page 24) – on Adams Old Colonial; Poached smoked haddock (page 21) – on Adams Veruschka

Fish

Fillets of sole véronique *(serves 1)*

2 fillets of sole
1 shallot or 2 slices of onion, chopped
3 small button mushrooms, sliced
½ bayleaf
salt and pepper
60ml (2fl oz) dry white wine
60ml (2fl oz) water
15g (½oz) butter
15g (½oz) plain flour
1 tablespoon single cream or top of the milk
50g (2oz) seedless grapes, skinned and halved

1 Wash the fish and pat dry with kitchen paper.
2 Arrange the fillets side by side in a shallow ovenproof dish.
3 Add the shallot or onion, mushrooms, bayleaf, seasoning, wine and water.
4 Cover and microwave on HIGH for 3 min or until fish flakes easily when tested with a fork.
5 Remove bayleaf, drain fish, reserving the liquor, and cover to keep warm.
6 Place the butter in a Pyrex jug and melt on HIGH for 30 sec.
7 Stir in flour and gradually blend in the cooling liquor and whisk until smooth.
8 Cook on HIGH for 2 min or until sauce has boiled and thickened, stirring every 1 min.
9 Stir in the cream with most of the grapes. Season to taste.
10 Pour sauce over fish and serve garnished with remaining grapes. If necessary reheat on HIGH for 1 min before serving.

VARIATION
Fillets of plaice Véronique: use 150–225g (6–8oz) plaice fillets instead of sole and proceed as above.

Breakfast kippers *(serves 2)*

1×198g (7oz) pack frozen buttered kipper fillets
scrambled eggs, using 2–4 eggs

1 Make a 2.5cm (1in) slit in the top of the bag of kipper fillets and place bag on a serving plate.
2 Microwave on HIGH for 6 min, rotating the plate after 3 min if the oven does not have a turntable.
3 Shake the bag gently and leave to stand, covered with another serving plate, while making scrambled eggs.
4 Divide the kippers and eggs between the two serving plates which will have been warmed by the kippers. Serve immediately.

VARIATION
Whole kipper for one: place a whole kipper, not frozen, on a serving plate. Cover with plastic wrap and microwave on HIGH for 1½–2 min, depending on size. Leave to stand, covered, for 2 min to finish cooking. Serve on its own or with scrambled eggs, cooked while the fish is standing.

Convenient fish'n'chips *(serves 1)*

1 pack oven crispy fish'n'chips, frozen

1 Preheat a microwave browning dish or griddle according to manufacturer's instructions.
2 Quickly place the fish and chips on the heated surface, pressing the fish portion well to make good contact.
3 Microwave on HIGH for 3 min.
4 Quickly turn fish and chips over and continue cooking on HIGH for a further 4 min or until cooked.
5 Serve immediately.

Note: *The actual time taken to brown and cook frozen foods will be affected by the freezer storage temperature.*

VARIATION

1 **Frozen fish cakes** (pack of 2): brush the fish cakes on both sides with vegetable oil and proceed as above to step 2. Microwave on HIGH for 2 min, turn fish cakes over and cook for a further 2–2½ min (see note above).

2 **Frozen fish fingers** (4): brush the fish fingers on both sides with vegetable oil and proceed as above. Microwave on HIGH for 1½ min, turn fingers over and cook for a further 1–2 min (see note).

3 **Frozen oven chips** (150–225g/6–8oz): place the oven chips in a single layer on the pre-heated browning dish. Microwave on HIGH for 2–2½ min. Turn chips over and cook for a further 2½–3 min (see note).

Plaice with mushroom sauce *(serves 1)*

150g (6oz) plaice fillets, skinned
15g (½oz) soft margarine
15g (½oz) plain flour
150ml (¼ pint) milk
3 button mushrooms
salt and pepper
1 teaspoon chopped parsley

1 Roll up the fillets from tail to head or fold in three and place in a shallow dish.

2 Cover and cook on HIGH for 3 min. Set aside, covered, to keep warm.

3 Place margarine, flour and milk into a Pyrex jug and whisk all well together.

4 Microwave on HIGH for 3 min or until sauce has boiled and thickened. Whisk every min.

5 Stir in mushrooms and cook on HIGH for a further 1 min.

6 Season to taste, stir in parsley and pour sauce over fish.

VARIATION

Haddock with mushroom sauce: use 150g (6oz) filleted, unsmoked haddock instead of plaice and proceed as above.

Poached smoked haddock *(serves 1)*

150–225g (6–8oz) smoked haddock
2 tablespoons milk
knob of butter
pepper

1 Place fish in a shallow serving dish and spoon milk on top.

2 Flake knob of butter on top of fish, and sprinkle with pepper.

3 Cover with plastic wrap and microwave on HIGH for 3–4 min, depending on weight and thickness of fish. Do not overcook.

4 Leave to stand, covered, for 2 min.

5 Serve either on its own with wholemeal bread to soak up the cooking juices, or topped with a poached or baked egg.

Note: *For 2 servings, double the above ingredients and cook on* HIGH *for 5 min or until fish flakes when tested with a fork. Do not overcook.*

Cod niçoise *(serves 2)*

1 tablespoon vegetable oil
1 medium onion, peeled and finely chopped
1 clove garlic, crushed
2 teaspoons chopped parsley
1 × 227g (8oz) can tomatoes, drained and roughly chopped
150ml (¼pt) dry white wine
salt and pepper
2 cod steaks, each weighing about 225g (8oz)
2 black olives

1 Place oil, onion and garlic in a Pyrex jug.

2 Cover and microwave on HIGH for 1½ min.

3 Stir in the parsley, tomatoes, wine and seasoning. Cover and cook on HIGH for 2 min.

4 Lay the cod steaks side by side in a shallow serving dish.

5 Pour sauce over fish. Cover and cook on HIGH for 6 min, turning dish after 3 min if the oven does not have a turntable.

6 Leave to stand, covered, for 2 min.

7 Place a black olive in the centre of each steak before serving.

Salmon steak en papillote *(serves 1)*

1 × 150g (6oz) salmon steak
a 30cm (12in) square of buttered greaseproof
    paper
50g (2oz) peeled prawns, defrosted if frozen
lemon juice
freshly ground black pepper
4 thin slices cucumber

1 Place salmon steak in the centre of the buttered greaseproof paper.
2 Fill the salmon cavity with prawns and sprinkle with lemon juice and pepper.
3 Lay overlapping slices of cucumber on top.
4 Fold the greaseproof paper over the fish and twist the ends to seal.
5 Place on a serving plate and microwave on HIGH for 2½ min or until salmon flesh flakes easily. Do not overcook. Test after 2 min. Stand for 2 min.
6 Serve hot with boiled new potatoes and 2 green vegetables.

Note: *Can be served cold with salad. Leave to cool wrapped in the greaseproof paper. This keeps the salmon moist.*

Cheesy fish pie *(serves 1)*

1 × 170g (6oz) pack cod in mushroom sauce,
    frozen
50g (2oz) button mushrooms, sliced
1 rasher bacon, de-rinded and chopped
100g (4oz) left-over mashed potato
2 tablespoons grated cheese
chopped parsley

1 Pierce a hole in the top of the bag of fish and place in a serving dish.
2 Microwave on LOW for 6 min. Stand for 2 min and then cook on LOW for a further 5 min. Leave to stand for 2 min.
3 Meanwhile place mushrooms and bacon in a dish.
4 Cover and microwave on HIGH for 2 min.
5 Turn the fish and sauce out of the bag and mix it together in a shallow dish using a fork.
6 Spread fish mixture over the bottom of the dish.
7 Top with cooked mushrooms and bacon.
8 Pipe or spoon the mashed potato around the outside of the dish and sprinkle the grated cheese over the centre.
9 Microwave on HIGH for about 2 min until heated through to centre.
10 Brown under a preheated conventional grill, if preferred, before sprinkling with chopped parsley.

VARIATION
Fish and vegetable pie: use any variety 170g (6oz) pack frozen fish in sauce. Replace mushrooms and bacon with 100g (4oz) leftover cooked vegetables. Proceed as above, heating the vegetables, covered, on HIGH for 1 min at step 4.

Store-cupboard crispy tuna *(serves 2)*

1 × 140g (4.9oz) can condensed cream of
    chicken or cream of mushroom soup,
    undiluted
1 × 198g (7oz) can tuna fish, drained and flaked
1 × 213g (7½oz) can button mushrooms in brine,
    drained and sliced
2 medium tomatoes, sliced
1 × 25g (0.88oz) packet potato crisps, crushed
2 tablespoons mature cheese, grated

1 Heat soup in a 600ml (1 pint) jug on HIGH for 1½ min, stirring after 45 sec.
2 Place the tuna in the bottom of a shallow dish and cover with sliced mushrooms.
3 Arrange tomato slices on top and pour over the soup.
4 Top with crushed crisps, mixed with cheese.
5 Microwave on HIGH for 1½–2 min or until cheese has melted and mixture has heated through to centre.
6 Sprinkle with paprika, or brown under a preheated conventional grill.

Store-cupboard crispy tuna (above); Sweetcorn (page 41); Fruited sponge pudding (page 56); Custard (page 18) – on Micratex Summer Delight

Soused herrings *(serves 2)*

2 medium herrings, heads removed
salt and pepper
1 medium onion, peeled and thinly sliced into
   rings
4 peppercorns
1 bay leaf
75ml (2½fl oz) cider or white wine vinegar
75ml (2½fl oz) water

1 Clean and bone the fish. Remove fins (or ask
   fishmonger to do it).
2 Place, skin side down, on a work surface.
   Sprinkle flesh with salt and pepper.
3 Roll up from head to tail and secure with
   wooden cocktail sticks.
4 Arrange side by side in a small dish or casserole so that they fit snugly together and
   have their tails pointing upwards.
5 Add the onion rings, peppercorns and
   bayleaf.
6 Mix the vinegar with the water and pour over
   the fish.
7 Cover and microwave on HIGH for 5 min,
   rotating the dish after 3 min if the oven does
   not have a turntable.
8 Leave to cool in the cooking liquid and then
   refrigerate.
9 Drain fish and remove cocktail sticks before
   serving cold with crusty or wholemeal bread
   and salad.

VARIATION
Use mackerel and proceed as above.

Baked trout *(serves 1)*

1 trout, cleaned, head and tail left on, weighing
   150–225g (6–8oz)
½ lemon
watercress

1 Wipe and dry trout, inside and out, with
   kitchen paper.
2 Slit the skin diagonally three times on each
   side.
3 Place the fish on a plate and sprinkle the juice
   of ¼ lemon over it, reserving the other ¼ for
   garnish.
4 Protect the tail and eye by covering with small
   pieces of smooth foil, if your oven manufacturer allows. Foil must not touch any part of
   the oven indicator.
5 Cover with plastic wrap and cook on HIGH for
   4 min or until fish flakes easily when tested
   with a fork. Rotate plate after 2 min if oven
   does not have a turntable.
6 Leave to stand, covered, for 2 min.
7 Remove foil and garnish with lemon wedges
   and watercress. Serve with salad.

Note: *2 trout will require a total cooking time of
6–8 min on* HIGH, *actual time will depend on
weight of fish. Place the fish side by side, head to
tail, in a shallow dish. Proceed as above but
rotate dish every 2 min if the oven does not have
a turntable and allow to stand for 4 min before
serving.*

Meat and poultry

Corned beef hash *(serves 1)*

1 × 225g (8oz) potato
1 small onion, peeled and chopped
100g (4oz) corned beef, cut into small pieces
salt and pepper

1 Wash and dry potato. Prick skin all over with a fork.
2 Place on a piece of kitchen paper on the oven floor or turntable and microwave on HIGH for 3 min.
3 Turn potato over and continue cooking on HIGH for a further 3 min. Leave to stand for a few minutes.
4 Meanwhile place onion with 2 teaspoons water in a small bowl. Cover and cook on HIGH for 1½ min. Drain.
5 Skin and mash or dice the potato and mix with the onion.
6 Stir in the corned beef and season to taste.
7 Spread the hash in an even layer on a plate, cover with plastic wrap and heat on HIGH for about 1–1½ min.
8 Serve with baked beans.

Note: *Use diced or mashed leftover cooked potato instead of cooking a jacket potato. The heating time at step 7 would then need to be extended slightly to heat the cold potato.*

VARIATIONS
Corned beef hash with cheese: mix 25g (1oz) grated cheese with potato and onion and sprinkle top with a further 25g (1oz) grated cheese at step 7. Brown under a preheated conventional grill.
Curried corned beef hash: stir in ½ teaspoon curry paste at step 5. Also add a skinned tomato, roughly chopped, and a tablespoon of sultanas. Serve with curried baked beans with sultanas.

Chilli con carne *(serves 1)*

1 small onion, peeled and finely chopped
1 small clove garlic, crushed
½ small green or red pepper, de-seeded and finely chopped
100g (4oz) lean minced beef, crumbled
2 tablespoons tomato chutney, relish or purée
½ teaspoon chilli powder or to taste
1 × 227g (8oz) can red kidney beans, drained
2 tomatoes, skinned and chopped

1 Place onion, garlic and pepper in a casserole
2 Cover and microwave on HIGH for 3 min. Stir after 1½ min.
3 Stir in the minced beef, cover and cook on HIGH for 2 min.
4 Break down mince with a fork and stir well.
5 Stir in remaining ingredients, re-cover and cook on HIGH for a further 3 min.
6 Stir, re-cover and cook on LOW for a further 5 min.
7 Stand for 5 min, covered.
8 Serve with rice or pasta, accompanied by a crisp green salad.

Lamb chop piquant *(serves 1)*

1 lamb chump chop weighing about 150g (6oz)
Worcestershire or soy sauce
pinch of garlic powder
a little French mustard
15–25g (½–1oz) blue Stilton cheese, crumbled
paprika

1 Brush the chop all over with Worcestershire or soy sauce and place in a shallow dish.
2 Cover with kitchen paper and cook on HIGH for 2 min.
3 Turn chop over, sprinkle with garlic powder and spread with mustard.
4 Scatter the crumbled cheese on top and cook on HIGH for a further 2½ min or until chop is cooked.
5 Stand for 2 min.
6 Sprinkle with paprika before serving.

Grillsteak moussaka *(serves 2)*

1 medium aubergine weighing about 225g (8oz)
1×227g (8oz) pack of 2 frozen lamb grillsteaks
1 medium onion, peeled and finely chopped
1 tablespoon vegetable oil
1×227g (8oz) can tomatoes
salt and pepper
1 egg, beaten
1×150g (5.3oz) tub natural, unsweetened yoghurt
50g (2oz) grated Cheddar cheese

1 Slice the aubergine thinly, sprinkle with salt and set aside for half an hour. Rinse well and pat dry on kitchen paper.
2 Place the grillsteaks on a plate. Cover with kitchen paper and microwave on HIGH for 3 min.
3 Turn grillsteaks over, cover and continue cooking on HIGH for a further 3–4 min. Leave to stand, covered, to keep warm.
4 Place the onion and oil in a bowl or dish. Stir in aubergine and coat in oil.
5 Cover and microwave onion and aubergine on HIGH for 5–6 min or until tender, shaking the dish or stirring gently after every 2 min.
6 Place half the cooked aubergine slices and onion in the bottom of an ovenproof serving dish and lay the grillsteaks, crumbled if liked, on top.
7 Roughly chop the tomatoes and spread with their juice over the grillsteaks. Sprinkle with salt and pepper. Top with remaining aubergine and onion.
8 Cover dish and microwave on HIGH for 2 min or until heated through.
9 Mix the egg with the yoghurt and stir in most of the cheese.
10 Pour over the aubergine, sprinkle with remaining cheese and place under a pre-heated grill until topping is set and browned.
11 Serve with salad.

Note: *Although moussaka is traditionally made with lamb, 1×213g (7½oz) can of minced beef and onion can be substituted for the lamb grill-steaks. Simply omit steps 2 and 3 and proceed as above, extending the time taken to heat through at step 8 if necessary.*

Kidneys in red wine *(serves 1)*

1×170g (6oz) pack commercially frozen braised kidneys in gravy
1 small onion, peeled and finely chopped
25g (1oz) button mushrooms, sliced
2–3 tablespoons red wine
chopped parsley or chives

1 Make a 2.5cm (1in) slit in the bag of kidneys and place them on a plate.
2 Microwave on HIGH for 2 min.
3 Turn the kidneys and their sauce into a serving dish. Stir in the onion, mushrooms and wine.
4 Cover and microwave on HIGH for 5 min. Stand for 3 min.
5 Serve sprinkled with parsley, either on a bed of cooked rice or with a jacket potato.

Ham steaks with pineapple *(serves 2)*

2×100g (4oz) ham steaks
2 slices fresh or canned pineapple
watercress

1 Arrange the ham steaks in a shallow dish or on a plate.
2 Cover and microwave on HIGH for 3 min.
3 Turn the steaks over and place a pineapple ring on top of each.
4 Microwave, uncovered, on HIGH for a further 2 min. Do not overcook.
5 Leave to stand, covered with an upturned plate for 2 min to finish cooking before serving garnished with watercress.

VARIATION
Gourmet ham steaks for two: omit pineapple. Follow steps 1 and 2 above but cook, covered, on HIGH for 3½–4 min at step 2, turning steaks over after 2 min. Leave to stand, covered. Meanwhile bake or poach two eggs. Place the cooked ham steaks on toasted muffin halves, top with cooked eggs and pour over a little cheese sauce, quickly made using commercially prepared sauce granules and boiling water.

Ham steaks with pineapple (above); Peas (page 41); Lyonnaise potatoes (page 37); Kiwi trifle (page 52) – on Adams Old Colonial

Glazed gammon joint *(servings; see Note)*

1 × 1kg (2lb 4oz) unsmoked gammon joint
1 tablespoon clear honey or golden syrup
pinch of ground cinnamon, optional
½ teaspoon mustard powder
1 tablespoon dark brown or demerara sugar

1   Soak the joint overnight in cold water if it is thought to be salty. Drain and dry thoroughly with kitchen paper.
2   Place the joint in a roasting bag. Pierce the bag in at least three places and secure the end loosely with string or an elastic band.
3   Place on a microwave roasting rack in a dish to catch the juices.
4   Microwave on HIGH for 8 min.
5   Leave to stand for 15 min in the bag.
6   Remove joint from bag, carefully remove the rind and score the fat.
7   Mix together the remaining ingredients and spread over the fat.
8   Pour excess juices from the dish and replace the joint on the microwave roasting rack.
9   Microwave on HIGH for a further 8 min or until the internal temperature of the joint registers 80°C (175°F).
10   Cover joint with a tent of foil, shiny side in, and leave stand for 15 min.
11   Serve hot or cold.

Note:
1   *This is an ideal dish for one person living alone, or for two people, since it can be served hot, perhaps with parsley sauce, potatoes and vegetables one day, and the remainder cooled and stored in the refrigerator to serve on another day with salad or as a sandwich filling. Useful to have over a holiday period.*
2   *If you do not have a microwave roasting rack use an upturned saucer or plate in a dish to catch juices.*

VARIATION
Glazed bacon joint: select an unsmoked bacon joint and proceed as for gammon joint but allow 9–10 min per 450g (1lb) total cooking time. Leave to stand for 10 min at step 5. At the end of the cooking period the internal temperature should read 80°C (175°F).

Gammon slice with orange sauce *(serves 1)*

1 slice of gammon or a gammon steak weighing about 150g (6oz)
½ teaspoon finely grated orange rind
juice of 1 orange
1 teaspoon cornflour
2 teaspoons soft brown sugar
pinch of ground ginger

1   Snip the rind of the ham and place in a shallow dish, preferably raised on a microwave roasting rack.
2   Cover with kitchen paper and microwave on HIGH for 2½ min or until cooked. Remove paper and leave to stand, covered with a serving plate.
3   Meanwhile measure the orange juice and, if necessary, add water to make up to 60ml (2fl oz).
4   Blend the cornflour into the orange juice and stir in the orange rind, sugar and ginger.
5   Microwave on HIGH for 2 min or until sauce has boiled and thickened. Stir during cooking after 1 min and 1½ min.

Note: *2 gammon portions will require approximately 4½ min at step 2 and the cooking dish should be rotated after 2 min if the oven does not have a turntable. Serve garnished with sliced peaches or mandarin orange segments, or make double quantity of orange sauce given above.*

Sausage and mash with baked beans *(serves 2)*

4 × 50g (2oz) pork or beef sausages
Worcestershire or soy sauce, optional
1 × 65g (2½oz) pack instant potato
240ml (8fl oz) water
60ml (2fl oz) milk
knob of butter
pepper
1 × 425g (15oz) can baked beans

1   Prick the sausages all over and place them, on a microwave roasting rack. To give colour, brush them with equal parts Worcestershire or soy sauce and water.

2 Cover with kitchen paper and microwave on HIGH for 2 min.

3 Turn sausages over, cover with kitchen paper and continue cooking on HIGH for a further 2 min. Leave to stand, covered, to keep warm.

4 Measure the water and milk into a Pyrex jug and stir in the instant potato, mixing with a fork.

5 Microwave on HIGH for 3 min, stirring after $1\frac{1}{2}$ min. Stir in butter and pepper to taste. Leave to stand, covered with a saucer.

6 Turn the baked beans into a bowl, cover and heat on HIGH for 2 min, stirring after 1 min.

Note: *If you do not have a microwave roasting rack place sausages around the outside of a medium size plate and proceed as above.*

Spicy spare ribs *(serves 1)*

225g (8oz) pork spare ribs
120ml (4fl oz) water
1 teaspoon vinegar
25g (1oz) butter
1 small onion, peeled and finely chopped
1 small clove garlic, crushed
1 tablespoon tomato ketchup
2 tablespoons chilli or soy sauce
2 teaspoons Worcestershire sauce
$\frac{1}{2}$ teaspoon made mustard
1 teaspoon lemon juice

1 Place the ribs with the water and vinegar in a casserole.

2 Cover and microwave on HIGH for 5 min or until meat is no longer pink. Drain and set aside, covered.

3 Place butter in a bowl or jug and microwave on HIGH for 45 sec. Add onion and garlic, cover and cook on HIGH for 2 min.

4 Stir in remaining ingredients, cover and microwave on HIGH for 1 min or until boiling.

5 Pour the sauce over the ribs, cover and microwave on LOW for about 4 min.

6 Turn ribs over, baste with sauce, cover and continue cooking on LOW for a further 4 min or until tender.

7 Serve with salad or rice, or simply with chunks of freshly baked bread

Minced beef *(serves 2)*

225g (8oz) lean minced beef
1 medium onion, peeled and finely chopped
2 teaspoons tomato purée
1 × 227g (8oz) can tomatoes
a good pinch of garlic salt
$\frac{1}{2}$ teaspoon dried mixed herbs
salt and pepper

1 Crumble the minced beef into a casserole and stir in the onion.

2 Cover and microwave on HIGH for 3 min. Stir and break up the mince with a fork after 2 min.

3 Stir in tomato purée and tomatoes, roughly chopped, with their juice, again breaking up mince with a fork. Stir in remaining ingredients.

4 Re-cover and continue cooking on HIGH for a further 5 min, stirring after 2 min.

5 Leave to stand, covered, for 2 min before serving with potatoes and vegetables.

Note: *All or half the above mixture can be used in the following recipes.*

VARIATIONS

1 **Spaghetti bolognese:** proceed as above and serve over hot cooked spaghetti, sprinkled with Parmesan cheese.

2 **Minced beef curry:** proceed as above, adding $\frac{1}{2}$ teaspoon curry paste or curry powder to taste at step 3. Peanuts, sultanas and/or leftover peas can also be added at this stage. Serve with fluffy, boiled rice, accompanied by any of the following – mango chutney, sliced banana, sliced tomatoes, chopped hardboiled egg, poppadums, desiccated coconut or raita (diced cucumber mixed with unsweetened natural yoghurt seasoned with salt, pepper and paprika).

3 **Cottage pie:** proceed as above to step 4. Stir in any leftover cooked vegetables and pipe or spread leftover cooked mashed potato evenly on top. Return to microwave and cook on HIGH for 2–3 min or until heated through. Place under a preheated grill for a crisp, brown top.

Browning dish brunch *(serves 1)*

2 sausages, preferably turkey with pork
2 rashers bacon
1–2 lambs' kidneys, skinned, halved and cored
1 tomato, halved

1 Preheat a microwave browning dish according to manufacturer's instructions.
2 Prick the sausages thoroughly all over and quickly place them in the preheated dish. Microwave on HIGH for 1½ min.
3 Snip bacon fat at regular intervals to prevent curling during cooking.
4 Turn the sausages over, add the bacon and kidney and microwave on HIGH for 1½ min.
5 Turn the sausages, bacon and kidney over, add the tomato halves and continue cooking on HIGH for a further 2 min or until all are cooked. Turn tomato halves over after 1 min.
6 Cover browning dish with its lid and leave to stand for 2–3 min before serving with toast, butter and marmalade.

Note: *To make a more substantial meal, serve with scrambled eggs or mushrooms which can be cooked during the standing time.*

Boeuf bourguignonne *(serves 2)*

2 rashers bacon, de-rinded and chopped
2 teaspoons plain flour
½ teaspoon instant beef flavour stock powder
pinch of thyme or basil
225g (8oz) lean braising steak, cut into cubes
1×227g (8oz) can tomatoes, roughly chopped
90ml (3fl oz) dry red wine
1 tablespoon brandy or water
12 tiny, frozen, whole onions, defrosted, or pickling onions
75g (3oz) button mushrooms, sliced
chopped parsley

1 Place bacon in an ovenproof casserole, cover and microwave on HIGH for 2 min.
2 Stir in flour, stock powder and herbs. Add steak, tomatoes with their juice, wine, brandy or water, and onions.

3 Cover and microwave on HIGH for 5 min, stirring after 2 and 4 min.
4 Reduce setting to LOW and cook for 20 min, stirring twice during this time.
5 Stir in mushrooms and continue cooking on LOW for a further 20 min or until meat is tender. Stir twice during this period.
6 Leave to stand, covered, for 5 min before serving, sprinkled with parsley.

Note: *As with conventionally cooked stews or casseroles this dish tastes even better if cooked the day before it is required. Cool and refrigerate overnight. Next day reheat, covered, on HIGH for 2–3 min or until just boiling. Stir gently twice during reheating.*

Slimmers' chicken casserole *(serves 2)*

2 boneless chicken breasts, each weighing 100–150g (4–6oz)
1×227g (8oz) can tomatoes
1 small onion, peeled and finely chopped
½ teaspoon dried mixed herbs
100g (4oz) sliced button mushrooms
salt and pepper
2 teaspoons freshly chopped parsley

1 Skin chicken and place in a casserole.
2 Drain the juice from the tomatoes and pour it over the chicken.
3 Add the onion and herbs, cover and microwave on HIGH for 8 min. Turn dish after 4 min if oven does not have a turntable.
4 Rearrange the chicken and baste with the juices. Chop the tomatoes roughly and add to the casserole with the mushrooms and seasoning.
5 Re-cover and continue cooking on HIGH for a further 4 min or until chicken is tender.
6 Leave to stand, covered, for 5 min before serving sprinkled with freshly chopped parsley.

Browning dish brunch (above); Mushrooms (page 40) – on Micratex Iris

Seasoned chicken joint *(serves 1)*

1 chicken leg joint weighing 225–275g
  (8–10oz)
microwave chicken seasoning or seasoned
  crumb mix

1 Skin joint, if preferred, and place on a plate.
  Sprinkle with microwave seasoning or coat in
  seasoned crumb mix.
2 Cover with kitchen paper and microwave on
  HIGH for 3 min.
3 Turn joint over and sprinkle with seasoning.
4 Cover with kitchen paper and continue
  cooking on HIGH for a further 3 min or until
  chicken is cooked and juices run clear.
5 Leave to stand, covered, for 5 min before
  serving, or brown and crisp under a preheated grill.

Stuffed roast chicken *(serves 2–3)*

1 small chicken weighing about 1.1kg (2lb 8oz),
  at room temperature, giblets removed
225g (8oz) pork sausagemeat
2 teaspoons chopped parsley
1 shallot or ½ small onion, finely chopped
1 tablespoon wine
microwave seasoned browning for chicken,
  optional

1 Wash chicken inside and outside and dry
  thoroughly with kitchen paper.
2 Mix the next four ingredients together to
  make stuffing.
3 Pack the stuffing, not too tightly, into the
  the neck end of the chicken and secure the
  skin flap in position with wooden cocktail
  sticks.
4 Place any remaining stuffing in body cavity.
5 Truss the chicken so that legs and wings are
  held close to the body to give a compact
  shape.
6 If allowed by your oven manufacturer, wing
  tips and leg ends may be shielded with small
  pieces of smooth aluminium foil to prevent
  overcooking. Foil must not touch any part
  of oven interior.

7 Weigh the stuffed chicken and calculate the
  total cooking time, allowing 7 min per 450g
  (1lb).
8 Sprinkle chicken all over with microwave
  seasoned browning, if used, and place,
  breast side down, either on an upturned
  saucer or plate, or on a microwave roasting
  rack, in an ovenproof dish to catch the
  juices.
9 Cover with a split roasting bag and microwave on HIGH for half the calculated cooking time.
10 Turn chicken over, breast side up; pour
  away excess juices from the dish and retain
  for gravy. Cook for remainder of time or
  until a meat thermometer inserted in the
  thickest part of each thigh registers 85°C
  (185°F) and juices run clear.
11 Leave to stand, outside the oven, loosely
  covered with foil, shiny side in, for 10–15
  min before serving.

Note:
1 *After standing time, breast of chicken can be
  browned by placing the bird under a preheated conventional grill.*
2 *Skin can be brushed with melted butter
  before, or instead of, sprinkling with microwave seasoned browning.*
3 *The cooking juices can simply be strained to
  serve with the hot chicken, or they can be
  used to make gravy.*
4 *Depending on quantity, any leftover chicken
  can either be served cold with salad or used in
  Chicken risotto or Chicken curry.*

VARIATION

Roast poussin (serves 1): a poussin weighs between 450–675g (1–1½lb) and is ideal for one
person. Proceed as for stuffed roast chicken,
halving the ingredients for the stuffing which is
placed in the body cavity. Allow 10 min per
450g (1lb), starting off breast side down and
turning the poussin breast side up after half the
cooking time. To give colour, skin can be
brushed before and during cooking with 2 teaspoons of honey and orange juice mixed
together. Alternatively brush with melted butter
mixed with a little Worcestershire sauce.

Chicken curry *(serves 1)*

15g (½oz) butter
½ small onion, finely chopped
1 teaspoon curry powder or to taste
15g (½oz) plain flour
150ml (5fl oz) chicken stock
few drops of Worcestershire sauce
1 teaspoon tomato ketchup
2 teaspoons mango chutney
½ teaspoon lemon juice
1 small dessert apple, peeled, cored and
    chopped
1 tablespoon sultanas or raisins
75–100g (3–4oz) cooked chicken meat, cubed
salt and pepper
1 tablespoon roasted peanuts

1 Place butter with the onion in a casserole.
2 Cover and microwave on HIGH for 1 min.
3 Stir in curry powder and flour, then gradually blend in the stock.
4 Re-cover and microwave on HIGH for 2 min or until sauce has boiled and thickened. Stir every minute.
5 Stir in Worcestershire sauce, tomato ketchup, chutney, lemon juice, apple and sultanas or raisins.
6 Cover and microwave on HIGH for 2 min.
7 Stir in chicken, cover and microwave on HIGH for a further 2 min.
8 Season to taste and leave to stand, covered, for 2 min.
9 Stir in peanuts or sprinkle them on top before serving with fluffy boiled rice, accompanied by any of the following – sliced tomatoes, sliced bananas, desiccated coconut, mango chutney, poppadums, chopped hard-boiled egg or raita (diced cucumber mixed with a little unsweetened natural yoghurt and seasoned with salt, freshly ground black pepper and a good pinch of paprika).

Note: *The flavour of curry improves if it is prepared the day before it is required. Cool and refrigerate. Reheat when required, covered, on HIGH for 2 min or until just boiling. Stir during reheating and serve as recommended above.*

Tropical turkey *(serves 2)*

1 fresh pineapple
25g (1oz) butter
1 small onion, peeled and finely chopped
2 tablespoons chopped green pepper
2 tablespoons chopped red pepper
100g (4oz) mushrooms, sliced
150g (6oz) cooked turkey meat, chopped
2 tablespoons wine vinegar
2 teaspoons demerara sugar
2 level teaspoons cornflour
120ml (4fl oz) turkey or chicken stock
dash of soy sauce
salt and pepper

1 Cut the pineapple in half top to bottom. Carefully remove the flesh and reserve the shells.
2 Chop the flesh, removing the core.
3 Place butter, onion and peppers in a bowl or casserole.
4 Cover and microwave on HIGH for 2½ min, stirring after 1½ min.
5 Stir in mushrooms, cover and cook on HIGH for a further 2 min.
6 Stir in the chopped pineapple and turkey.
7 Blend the vinegar and sugar with the cornflour in a Pyrex jug. Gradually stir in the stock.
8 Microwave on HIGH for 2 min or until sauce has boiled and thickened. Stir after 1 and 1½ min.
9 Stir into the turkey mixture. Add the soy sauce and season to taste.
10 Cover and microwave on HIGH for 3 min, stirring gently after 1½ min.
11 Divide the mixture between the half pineapple shells.
12 Place the filled shells in a deep serving dish.
13 Cover with plastic wrap and microwave on HIGH for about 1–1½ min to warm the shells before serving.

Note: *This is virtually a meal in itself and needs no more than a side salad as an accompaniment. It is a rather unusual, attractive and delicious main course to serve for that special occasion.*

Vegetables

Cauliflower with blue cheese sauce
(serves 1)

1 × 225g (8oz) pack frozen cauliflower florets
4 tablespoons water
1½ level teaspoons cornflour
98ml (3fl oz) milk
50g (2oz) Blue Stilton, Blue Cheshire or Danish Blue cheese, crumbled
salt and pepper
25g (1oz) roasted peanuts, preferably coarsely chopped

1 Place the cauliflower and water in a serving dish.
2 Cover and microwave on HIGH for 7 min or until tender but crisp. Drain cauliflower, reserving liquid, and cover to keep warm.
3 Blend the cornflour with a little of the milk to give a smooth paste.
4 Stir in remainder of milk and 60ml (2fl oz) of reserved cooking liquor.
5 Microwave on HIGH for 2 min or until sauce has boiled and thickened. Stir or whisk after 1 min and 1½ min.
6 Stir in crumbled cheese and season to taste.
7 Pour sauce over cauliflower and if necessary reheat on HIGH for about 1 min.
8 Sprinkle with peanuts before serving with a jacket potato as a meatless main course, accompanied perhaps by a side salad.

VARIATION
Cauliflower and blue cheese soup: any leftover cauliflower with sauce can be mixed with a little milk or chicken stock and sieved, or puréed in a blender or food processor, to give a creamy thick tasty soup. Turn into a soup bowl and heat on HIGH, for 2 min, stirring after 1 min. Serve with croûtons.

Ratatouille *(serves 1–2)*

100g (4oz) aubergine, cut into 1.25cm (½in) slices
salt
1 small clove garlic, crushed or finely chopped
1 small onion, peeled, sliced and separated into rings
1 tablespoon vegetable oil
1 small courgette, sliced
¼ red pepper, de-seeded and cut into thin strips
¼ green pepper, de-seeded and cut into thin strips
225g (8oz) skinned tomatoes, fresh or canned, roughly chopped
2 teaspoons tomato purée
freshly ground black pepper
pinch of dried basil and thyme
chopped chives or parsley

1 Sprinkle the sliced aubergine with salt and set aside for 30 min. Rinse well, drain and pat dry on kitchen paper. Cut into cubes.
2 Place the garlic, onion and oil in a bowl or casserole.
3 Cover with a tight-fitting lid or plastic wrap and cook on HIGH for 1½ min.
4 Stir in remaining ingredients, except chives or parsley.
5 Cover and continue cooking on HIGH for a further 10 min or until all vegetables are tender.
6 Sprinkle with chopped chives or parsley and serve hot as a vegetable with meat, poultry or fish or cold as a starter or salad.

Note: *The above recipe can be served on its own as a main course dish to serve one or two. After step 5, sprinkle with 50g (2oz) grated mozzarella, Emmenthal, Gruyère or mature Cheddar cheese and microwave for 1 min or until cheese has melted. Sprinkle with chopped chives, parsley or paprika before serving with crusty bread to mop up the juices.*

Ratatouille (above); Cauliflower with blue cheese sauce (above); Baked jacket potato (page 40) – on Micratex Bluebell

Vegetarian casserole *(serves 1)*

100g (4oz) carrots, scraped and sliced into rings or matchsticks
100g (4oz) cauliflower florets
1 small onion, peeled and finely sliced
1 stick celery, chopped
2 tablespoons tomato juice, dry white wine or water
2 tablespoons dry brown breadcrumbs
25g (1oz) grated cheese
1 hard-boiled egg, finely chopped or 25g (1oz) toasted flaked almonds
chopped parsley

1 Place the vegetables and liquid into a flame-proof casserole, cover with a tight-fitting lid and cook on HIGH for 7 min or until vegetables are tender. Stir after 3 min.

2 Mix the breadcrumbs with most of the cheese and sprinkle over vegetables. Top with remaining cheese.
3 Place under a preheated conventional grill for a crisp brown topping. Alternatively, return to microwave oven and cook on HIGH for about 1 minute to melt cheese. Stand for 2 min.
4 Garnish with chopped hard-boiled egg or toasted flaked almonds and parsley before serving.

Note:
1 *For 2 servings, double the above quantities and cook for about 10 min at step 1.*
2 *This is a useful way of using up small quantities of raw vegetables, and ingredients can be varied accordingly. Select vegetables which require approximately the same length of cooking. Increasing or decreasing the total weight will alter the cooking time.*

Guide to cooking fresh vegetables

When cooking fresh or frozen vegetables for one person, either cook enough for two meals, or cook small quantities of two or more different vegetables at the same time. The total uncooked weight of vegetables, excluding potatoes, to accompany a main course, will normally be about 225g (8oz) per person. Select vegetables which require approximately the same cooking time, and either cook them in the same or separate roasting bags or covered serving dishes. Remember to calculate the overall cooking time according to the total weight of vegetables.

Place the fresh vegetables with 4 tablespoons water, unless otherwise stated, in a covered dish.

Vegetable	Quantity	Approximate Time on HIGH Setting	Special Instructions
Aubergines, sliced	1 medium	6–7 min	Stir during cooking; stand 3 min before serving
Beans			
broad, shelled	225g (8oz)	5–6 min	Stir during cooking; stand 3 min before serving
runner, sliced	225g (8oz)	6–7 min	Stir during cooking; stand 2–3 min before serving
Broccoli spears	225g (8oz)	6–8 min	Place stalks towards outside of dish; rearrange during cooking

Vegetarian casserole (above); Baked stuffed apple (page 54) – on Micratex Summer Delight

Guide to cooking fresh vegetables

Vegetable	Quantity	Approximate Time on HIGH Setting	Special Instructions
Brussels sprouts	225g (8oz)	5–6 min	Cut a cross in stalk end; stir during cooking; stand 2–3 min before serving
Cabbage, shredded	225g (8oz)	6–7 min	Stir during cooking; stand 2–3 min before serving
Carrots, sliced	225g (8oz)	7–8 min	Stir during cooking; stand 3 min before serving
Cauliflower florets	225g (8oz) 450g (1lb)	6–7 min 10–11 min	Stir during cooking; stand 2–3 min before serving
Celery, sliced	225g (8oz)	6–7 min	Stir during cooking; stand 3 min before serving
Corn-on-the-cob	1 cob 2 cobs	3–4 min 6–8 min	Wrap individually in buttered greaseproof paper, no water; turn over during cooking
Courgettes, sliced	225g (8oz)	6–7 min	Do not add water; stir during cooking; stand 3 min before serving
Leeks, sliced	225g (8oz)	6–7 min	Stir or shake during cooking; stand 3 min before serving
Mushrooms	100g (4oz) 225g (8oz)	1–2 min 3–4 min	Do not add water; cook in 25g (1oz) butter; stir during cooking
Onions, sliced	225g (8oz)	5–7 min	Stir or shake during cooking
Parsnips, sliced	225g (8oz)	7–8 min	Stir during cooking; stand 3 min before serving
Peas	100g (4oz) 225g (8oz)	4–5 min 7–9 min	Stir during cooking; stand 2 min before serving
Potatoes, jacket	1×225g (8oz) 2×225g (8oz)	6 min 9–10 min	Prick skin; place on kitchen paper; turn over during cooking; stand for 5 min before serving
boiled	450g (1lb)	10 minutes	Cut into 25g (1oz) pieces; shake or stir during cooking; stand 3 min before serving
Spinach	225g (8oz)	4–5 min	Do not add water; stir during cooking
Swede/Turnip, diced	225g (8oz)	7–9 min	Stir during cooking, time will vary with age; stand 5 min; drain and mash before serving

Guide to cooking frozen vegetables

When cooking fresh or frozen vegetables for one person, either cook enough for two meals, or cook small quantities of two or more different vegetables at the same time. The total uncooked weight of vegetables, excluding potatoes, to accompany a main course, will normally be about 225g (8oz) per person. Select vegetables which require approximately the same cooking time, and either cook them in the same or separate roasting bags or covered serving dishes. Remember to calculate the overall cooking time according to the total weight of vegetables.

Place the frozen vegetables with 4 tablespoons water, unless otherwise stated, in a covered dish.

Vegetable	Quantity	Approximate Time on HIGH Setting	Special Instructions
Asparagus spears	225g (8oz)	6–7 min	Separate spears during cooking; stand 2 min before serving
beans			
broad	225g (8oz)	8 min	Stir or shake during cooking; stand 3 min before serving
green, sliced or whole	225g (8oz)	7–8 min	Stir during cooking; stand 2–3 min before serving
Broccoli spears	225g (8oz)	8–9 min	Rearrange spears during cooking; stand 2–3 min before serving
Brussels sprouts	225g (8oz)	6–7 min	Stir or shake during cooking; stand 2 min before cooking
Carrots	225g (8oz)	7–8 min	Stir or shake during cooking; stand 2 min before serving
Corn-on-the-cob	1 cob	4 min	Wrap in buttered greaseproof paper, no water; turn over during cooking
	2 cobs	7 min	
Mixed vegetables, diced	225g (8oz)	5–6 min	Stir during cooking; stand 2 min before serving
Peas	100g (4oz)	3 min	Stir or shake during cooking; stand 2 min before serving
Peas with baby carrots	283g (10oz) pack	5 min	Stir during cooking; stand 2 min before serving
Spinach, chopped or cut leaf	300g (10½oz) pack	9 min	Do not add water, add a knob of butter; stir during cooking; stand 2 min before serving
Sprouts with cauliflower and baby carrots	283g (10oz) pack	9 min	Stir during cooking; stand 2 min before serving
Sweetcorn with peas and carrots	283g (10oz) pack	7 min	Stir during cooking; stand 2 min before serving

Rice, pasta and grains

Boiled long-grain rice *(serves 2)*

300ml (½pt) boiling water or boiling chicken
  stock
100g (4oz) long-grain rice
½ teaspoon salt
1 teaspoon vegetable oil

1 Pour the boiling water or stock into a large
  bowl or casserole.
2 Stir in rice, salt and oil.
3 Cover and microwave on HIGH for 2 min or
  until water returns to a rolling boil.
4 Reduce to LOW and continue cooking for a
  further 12 min. Stir at least once during cooking.
5 Leave to stand, covered, for 5 min.
6 Fluff up with a fork to separate grains before
  serving.

Note:
1 *If you find that the rice will not simmer on
  LOW setting on your oven, use HIGH setting
  throughout and cook as above for 12 min
  after the water returns to the boil.*
2 *Cooked rice reheats most successfully in a
  microwave oven. Simply place in a covered
  dish and heat on HIGH, allowing 1½ min for a
  single portion and 2 min for 2 portions.
  Therefore, even if cooking only for one, cook
  enough rice for 2 servings and store any leftover cooled rice in the refrigerator ready to
  reheat when required. Fluff up the reheated
  rice with a fork to separate grains before
  serving.*

VARIATION
Brown rice: use 450ml (¾pt) boiling water or
stock and proceed as above to step 3. After
water has returned to the boil, either reduce
setting to LOW or continue on HIGH for about a
further 20 min, stirring at least once during this
time. Leave to stand, covered, for at least 5 min
before fluffing up with a fork to serve.
Remember that brown rice has a slightly chewy
texture and is never as soft as white rice.

Ham and mushroom risotto *(serves 1)*

50g (2oz) long-grain rice
150ml (5fl oz) boiling chicken stock made with
  instant chicken-flavour stock powder and
  boiling water
knob of butter
1 small onion, peeled and finely chopped
1 tablespoon chopped green pepper
1 tablespoons water
50g (2oz) button mushrooms, sliced or chopped
100g (4oz) cooked ham, chopped
1 tablespoon grated cheese
salt and pepper
soy sauce

1 Place the rice, stock and butter in a bowl large
  enough to prevent boiling over during cooking.
2 Cover and microwave on HIGH for 2 min or
  until boiling. Reduce to LOW and cook for a
  further 12 min or until rice is cooked and
  water has been absorbed. Leave to stand.
3 Place the onion, green pepper and water in a
  covered dish and microwave on HIGH for 2
  min. Drain.
4 Stir in the rice, mushrooms, ham and cheese.
  Season to taste.
5 Cover and microwave on HIGH for 3 min or
  until cheese has melted and mixture has
  heated through to centre.
6 Serve sprinkled with soy sauce.

Note: *If brown rice is used, extend cooking time
on LOW by about 8 min at stage 2.*

VARIATION
Chicken, sausage, frankfurter or tuna risotto:
instead of ham use any of the above cooked
meats or a small can of tuna fish.

*Ham and mushroom risotto (above); Macaroni with
cheese and ham (page 45); Quick fruit crumble (page
50) – on Micratex Florida*

Eggs and cheese

Scrambled eggs (serves 1)

15g (½oz) butter
2 eggs
2 tablespoons milk or water, or a mixture of
   both
salt and pepper
bread, toasted conventionally and buttered
cress

1 Melt the butter in a bowl or jug on HIGH for
   30 sec.
2 Add the eggs, milk and seasoning, and beat
   all together.
3 Microwave on HIGH for 1½–2 min, depending
   on preferred consistency. Stir every 30 sec.
   Do not overcook. Remove eggs from the oven
   while they are still soft and moist. If after
   standing they are not cooked sufficiently for
   your liking, simply return them to the oven
   and cook on HIGH for a further 10–15 seconds.
4 Stand for about a minute to finish cooking.
   Stir before serving.
5 Serve on hot buttered toast, garnished with
   cress.

Note:
1 *Omit butter if slimming, or on a low-fat diet.*
2 *For 2 servings use 4 eggs and 4 tablespoons
   milk. Proceed as above and cook for about 3
   min.*

VARIATIONS
Prawn scramble (serves 1–2): stir in 50 or 100g
(2 or 4oz) peeled prawns for the final minute of
the above cooking times.
Bacon and egg scramble (serves 1–2): cook 2 or
4 rashers of bacon and leave to stand, covered,
while cooking eggs. Chop the cooked bacon and
stir into the eggs for the final minute of the
above cooking times.

Poached eggs (serves 1–2)

125ml (4fl oz) water
2 teaspoons vinegar
2 eggs, at room temperature

1 Select two small dishes and place 50ml (2fl
   oz) water and 1 teaspoon vinegar in each.
2 Microwave on HIGH for 2 min, or until boiling.
3 Carefully break the eggs into the dishes and
   pierce the yolks gently with a fork.
4 Microwave on HIGH for 1 min. Do not overcook.
5 Leave to stand, covered, for 2 min before
   draining and serving on hot buttered toast or
   toasted buttered muffins.

Note:
1 *Shake poached eggs gently during the standing time. This helps the white to set. Do not
   uncover until ready to serve.*
2 *To poach 1 egg, halve the ingredients. At step
   2, microwave on HIGH for 45–60 sec or until
   water boils, but at step 4 microwave on LOW
   for 1–1¼ min or until white is nearly set. Do
   not overcook. Leave to stand, covered, for
   about 2 min before serving as above.*

Baked eggs (serves 1–2)

2 eggs, at room temperature

1 Lightly butter two saucers or small individual
   dishes.
2 Break an egg into each, and pierce the yolk
   carefully with a fork.
3 Cover with plastic wrap and microwave on
   LOW for about 3¼–3¾ min, depending on personal preference. Do not overcook.
4 Leave to stand, covered, to finish cooking for
   1 min before serving.

VARIATION
Swiss eggs: lightly butter the insides of two individual dishes and sprinkle 2 teaspoons grated
cheese in each. Break an egg on top, pierce the
yolk and pour 1 tablespoon single cream over.
Sprinkle with a further 2 teaspoons grated
cheese and proceed as above from step 3. Serve
garnished with paprika.

*Chilli con carne (page 25); Tricolore Italian pasta
(see spaghetti page 44) – on Micratex Plain White*

Fruit and desserts

Chocolate rum mousse (serves 1)

50g (2oz) plain chocolate-flavoured cake
    covering
1 egg, separated
1–2 teaspoons rum as preferred
whipped cream and grated chocolate or
    chopped nuts

1 Break the chocolate cake covering into small
   pieces and place in a medium-sized bowl or
   jug.
2 Microwave on HIGH for 45 sec or until
   melted, stirring after 30 sec.
3 Beat in the egg yolk and rum. Leave mixture
   to cool slightly.
4 Meanwhile beat egg white until it reaches the
   soft peak stage and fold into the cooled
   chocolate mixture.
5 Pour into an individual dessert dish and
   refrigerate till set.
6 Serve topped with whipped cream and grated
   chocolate or chopped nuts.

Note: *for 2 servings, double the quantity of
ingredients and melt the chocolate or cake covering on* HIGH *for 1½–2 min or until melted,
stirring after 1 and 1½ min. Proceed as above.*

VARIATION
Chocolate orange mousse: omit rum. Stir in the
juice and finely grated rind of half an orange to
the 2-serving quantity at step 3 and proceed as
above. Decorate with confectioner's miniature
orange and lemon slices.

Quick fruit crumble (serves 1)

15g (½oz) butter
25g (1oz) digestive or gingerbread biscuits,
    crushed
150g (6oz) leftover stewed or canned fruit or pie
    filling

1 Place butter in a bowl and melt on HIGH for 30
   sec.
2 Using a fork, stir in the crushed biscuits until
   thoroughly coated in butter. Spread out on a
   flat plate and leave to cool.
3 Place the fruit or pie filling in an individual
   serving dish. Cover and heat on HIGH for 1
   min or until warm.
4 Sprinkle the crumbled biscuits on top and
   microwave on HIGH for a further 45 sec.
5 Leave to stand for 2 min before serving with
   cream, custard or ice-cream.

Jellied rhubarb (serves 2)

225g (8oz) rhubarb, cut into 2.5cm (1in) lengths
120ml (4fl oz) water
caster sugar or artificial sweetener to taste
½ a 142g (5oz) packet orange jelly cubes

1 Place rhubarb and water in a casserole.
2 Cover and cook on HIGH for 3 min or until
   rhubarb is tender but still holding its shape.
3 Strain rhubarb, reserving juice.
4 Place 150ml (¼pt) of the juice in a Pyrex
   measuring jug with the cut-up jelly cubes.
5 Microwave on HIGH for 2 min or until jelly is
   dissolved, stirring after 1 min.
6 Stir in remaining rhubarb juice and, if necessary, add water to make up to 300ml (½pt).
7 Add caster sugar to taste.
8 Divide the rhubarb between two individual
   dishes.
9 Pour jelly over rhubarb and refrigerate until
   set.
10 Serve plain or topped with yoghurt or
   cream.

Note:
1 *Fresh rhubarb is very low in calories but,
   since it needs to be cooked with rather a lot of
   sugar, its calorie count can soar. Using jelly as
   a sweetener is a pleasant way of reducing
   calories. Whether or not you add a little sugar
   or artificial sweetener will depend on flavour
   of rhubarb and personal preference.*
2 *To give variety try other combinations of
   fresh, frozen or canned fruits and flavoured
   jellies.*

*Spicy spare ribs (page 29); Sweet and sour savoury
rice (see long grain rice page 42); Chocolate rum
mousse (above) – on Adams Jenny Wren Collection*

Kiwi trifle *(serves 2)*

Cake base:
50g (2oz) soft tub margarine
50g (2oz) caster sugar
50g (2oz) self-raising flour
pinch of salt
1 egg
2 teaspoons warm water

lemon curd or raspberry jam
2 tablespoons brandy, white wine or orange
    juice
2 kiwi fruit, skinned and thinly sliced
½ packet instant custard powder
whipped cream
flaked almonds, chopped nuts or grated
    chocolate

1 Place all the cake-base ingredients in a mix-
    ing bowl and beat together for 2 min by
    hand, or for 1 min if using an electric food
    mixer.
2 Turn mixture into a greased 16.5cm (6½in)
    ovenproof flan dish, the base lined with
    greased greaseproof paper. Level the surface
    with a knife.
3 Microwave on HIGH for 2½ min or until
    cooked in centre. Leave to stand 2 min
    before turning out to cool.
4 When cold, cut in half vertically and set one
    half aside.
5 Split in half horizontally and spread with
    lemon curd or jam.
6 Cut into cubes and use enough to give a
    good layer in the base of two individual
    dishes.
7 Pour over enough brandy, wine or fruit juice
    to moisten the cake.
8 Arrange most of the kiwi slices on top of the
    sponge.
9 Make up half the instant custard, according
    to pack instructions, remembering to add
    only half the recommended quantity of boil-
    ing water.
10 Leave custard to cool slightly before pour-
    ing over the fruit. Cool and refrigerate.
11 When chilled, decorate with cream, remain-
    ing kiwi slices and flaked almonds, chopped
    nuts or grated chocolate.

Pineapple-upside-down pudding *(serves 2–4)*

25g (1oz) butter
50g (2oz) demerara or soft brown sugar
2–4 rings of fresh or drained canned pineapple,
    according to size
halved glacé cherries
50g (2oz) soft margarine
50g (2oz) caster sugar
50g (2oz) self-raising flour
pinch of salt
1 egg, beaten
2 teaspoons warm water or pineapple juice

1 Grease a straight-sided soufflé dish, at least
    900ml (1½pt) capacity, with the butter.
    Sprinkle with the demerara or soft brown
    sugar.
2 Microwave on HIGH for 45–60 sec.
3 Arrange the pineapple rings with the cherries
    in an attractive pattern over base of dish.
4 Place remaining ingredients, except water or
    juice, in a bowl and mix well together for 2
    min by hand or for 1 min using an electric
    food mixer. Stir in water or juice.
5 Spread mixture carefully over fruit and level
    the top.
6 Microwave on HIGH for 5 min or until only
    slightly moist on top and cooked in centre.
    Rotate dish after 2½ min if oven does not have
    a turntable.
7 Stand for 3 min before inverting onto a warm
    serving plate.
8 Serve with cream or ice-cream.

Note: *Any leftover portions can either be served
cold as a cake or reheated on HIGH for 30–45
sec.*

VARIATION
Chocolate-upside-down pudding: replace 15g
(½oz) of the flour with 15g (½oz) sieved cocoa and
proceed as above. Good with fresh or drained
canned pear halves or mandarin segments
instead of pineapple.

Raspberry delight *(serves 2–3)*

1 × 400g (14oz) can raspberries in fruit juice
3 level teaspoons cornflour
2 teaspoons brandy
150ml (¼pt) whipping cream
nutmeg
sponge fingers or boudoir biscuits

1 Drain the raspberries and blend the juice with the cornflour in a bowl or jug.
2 Microwave on HIGH for 2½ min or until boiling and thickened, stirring after 1½ min.
3 Stir in raspberries and brandy, mixing well together, and pour into individual serving glasses.
4 Leave to cool and refrigerate until required.
5 Decorate with whipped cream, dust with nutmeg, and serve with sponge fingers or boudoir biscuits.

Baked egg custards *(serves 2)*

300ml (½pt) milk
2 eggs, lightly beaten
1 tablespoon caster sugar
few drops of vanilla essence
grated or ground nutmeg

1 Place milk in a jug and microwave on HIGH for 1½ min. Do not allow to boil.
2 Add the beaten egg, sugar and essence. Beat all together.
3 Strain mixture into two individual serving dishes and sprinkle with nutmeg.
4 Place, apart, in the oven and microwave on LOW for 10 min or until custards are just set. Centres will not be quite firm. Do not overcook, or custard will curdle.
5 Leave to stand for at least 10 min before serving warm. Alternatively leave to cool, refrigerate for at least 2 hours, and serve chilled.

Note: *Even if only cooking for 1 person, it makes sense to make two individual custards at a time. The second can be stored in the refrigerator and served the following day, either as plain baked egg custard or as Crème brûlée (see Variation).*

VARIATION
Crème brûlée: proceed as above but omit nutmeg and cook the custard in an individual flameproof dish. Chill for at least 3 hours. Cover the top surface with a tablespoon of demerara or soft brown sugar and place under a preheated grill until sugar caramelises. Cool and chill for a further 2 hours before serving.

Bread and butter pudding
(serves 2 generously)

100g (4oz) stale bread
butter
50g (2oz) mixed dried fruit or chopped dates
good pinch of nutmeg
good pinch of cinnamon
1 scant tablespoon demerara or soft brown sugar
300ml (½pt) milk
1 large egg, beaten
caster sugar

1 Slice bread, remove crusts; spread slices with butter. Cut into small cubes.
2 Mix bread cubes with dried fruit, spices and sugar and place in a small ovenproof pie dish or casserole.
3 Heat milk in an ovenproof measuring jug for 1 min. Pour onto beaten egg and strain over bread mixture.
4 Press bread down into liquid with a fork and leave to soak for 20 min.
5 Microwave on LOW for 15 min or until just set in centre.
6 Leave to stand for 3 min and sprinkle with caster sugar before serving.

Note: *This is delicious made with stale hot cross buns, fruit teacakes, spiced buns or bunloaf. Where fruit is already incorporated in the buns or loaf, additional fruit is unnecessary. Spices may also be omitted and sugar can be reduced or left out.*

Apple and berry crunch (serves 1)

1 large dessert apple
2 tablespoons raspberries or blackberries
sugar if necessary
2 tablespoons bran breakfast flakes
1 tablespoon golden syrup or honey

1 Peel and core the apple. Slice fairly thickly and place in a serving dish.
2 Cover and microwave on HIGH for 2½–3 min, depending on size of apple.
3 Stir in berries and add sugar to taste if necessary.
4 Place the flakes and syrup or honey in a bowl. Mix well together and microwave on HIGH for 30 sec.
5 Spoon over fruit and serve either warm or chilled with ice-cream or cream.

Baked stuffed apple (serves 1)

1 medium-sized cooking apple
2–3 teaspoons mincemeat

1 Wash and dry the apple. Remove the core, prick the skin all over with a fork and place on a plate or in an individual serving dish.
2 Fill the cavity with mincemeat. Cover loosely with greased greaseproof paper.
3 Microwave on HIGH for 2½–3 min, depending on size. Apple should still be firm when removed from the oven.
4 Leave to stand, covered, for 2 min to finish cooking.
5 Baste with its own juices before serving.

Note:
1 *The speed of cooking may vary with the type, as well as the size, of apple used.*
2 *When cooking more than one apple at a time, leave a space of 2.5cm (1in) between each and arrange three or more in a circle around the outside of a suitable shallow round dish.*

VARIATION
Vary the filling by replacing the mincemeat with mixed dried fruit, dates, dates and nuts, or simply fill the centre with brown sugar, topped with a knob of butter.

Compôte of dried fruit (serves 3–4)

1 × 225g (8oz) pack mixed dried fruit (apricots, prunes, apples etc)
450ml (¾pt) water or a mixture of water and wine
25g (1oz) sugar, optional

1 Place the fruit with the liquid in a casserole.
2 Cover and microwave on HIGH for 6 min.
3 Stir, adding sugar if used, cover and cook on HIGH for a further 6 min.
4 Leave to stand, covered, for at least 30 min to completely re-hydrate.
5 Cool and refrigerate, preferably overnight. Stir before serving.

Note:
1 *This is a very versatile dish which can be served on its own or with cereal for breakfast, or as a dessert with or without cream, custard or ice-cream.*
2 *If softer fruit is preferred, soak in the liquid for at least 6 hours before cooking.*

Chocolate nutty pear (serves 2)

1 × 227g (8oz) can pear halves in apple juice, drained
1 Mars bar
1 tablespoon milk
2 teaspoons chopped nuts

1 Place the pear halves in an individual dessert dish.
2 Cut up Mars bar into small pieces and place in a small ovenproof bowl with the milk.
3 Microwave on HIGH for 1 min or until melted, stirring after every 30 sec.
4 Pour chocolate sauce over the pear halves and sprinkle with chopped nuts.

VARIATION
Pear belle Hélène (serves 2): make a sauce as given in steps 2 and 3 above. Place portions of vanilla or chocolate ice-cream in individual dessert dishes. Top each with a pear half. Pour sauce on top and sprinkle with nuts.

Cottage pie (page 29); Sliced carrots (page 40); Sliced green beans (page 38); Chocolate nutty pear (above) – on Adams Blue Daisy

Croissant St Clements (serves 1)

Lemon curd:
40g (1½oz) butter
75g (3oz) caster sugar
rind and juice of 1 large lemon
1 large egg, beaten

1 freshly baked baker's croissant
fresh orange, satsuma or clementine segments
2 tablespoons mandarin yoghurt
whipping cream for serving, optional

1 First make lemon curd. Place butter in a mixing bowl and microwave on HIGH for 1½ min or until melted.
2 Stir in sugar, lemon rind and strained lemon juice.
3 Microwave on HIGH for 2 min to dissolve sugar, stirring after 1 min.
4 Beat in egg and continue cooking on HIGH for 2½ min or until mixture is thick enough to coat the back of a spoon. Check and stir at least every minute.
5 Reserve 2 tablespoons and set aside to cool.
6 Pour remainder into a sterilised warm jar. Cover, seal and label in the usual way.
7 Split croissant in half horizontally and spread the cut surfaces with the cooled reserved lemon curd.
8 Arrange the fruit segments on the bottom half and spoon the yoghurt over the fruit.
9 Replace the top half of the croissant and serve with or without whipping cream.

Note:
1 *The remaining lemon curd should be stored in a refrigerator and used within a month, as a spread or in desserts. Try swirling a little curd through leftover whipped cream, yoghurt or fromage blanc to serve alone or with fruit as a quick dessert.*
2 *The croissant can be heated in the microwave but it will tend to lose its crispness. It must not be overheated or it will toughen. Place on kitchen paper or on a microwave roasting rack and heat on HIGH for about 20 sec.*

VARIATION
Dessert croissant: proceed as above to step 7. Fill with other fresh or canned fruit. Alternatively use leftover stewed fruit or pie filling.

Basic 'steamed' pudding (serves 2–3)

50g (2oz) soft margarine
50g (2oz) caster or soft brown sugar
50g (2oz) self-raising wholewheat or white flour
pinch of salt
1 egg, beaten
2 teaspoons warm water

1 Place margarine, sugar, flour, salt and egg in a bowl and mix together for 2 min by hand or for 1 min with an electric food mixer.
2 Stir in water.
3 Turn mixture into a greased 600ml (1pt) pudding basin or Pyrex measuring jug, the base lined with a circle of greased greaseproof paper. Smooth and level the top.
4 Microwave on HIGH for 3–3½ min or until pudding is slightly moist on top. Rotate container after 2 min if oven does not have a turntable.
5 Stand for 3 min before turning out to serve with custard or sauce.

Note: *Single portions of leftover pudding can be quickly reheated on* HIGH *in a serving dish in about 30–45 sec, depending on size of portion. Do not overheat.*

VARIATIONS (using a 900ml (1½pt) ovenproof pudding basin)
Fruited sponge pudding: proceed as above, stirring in 50g (2oz) currants, raisins or sultanas or 50g (2oz) mixed dried fruit with the water.
Ginger sponge pudding: proceed as above, adding ½ level teaspoon ground ginger at step 1 and 25g (1oz) chopped crystallised ginger with 1 teaspoon black treacle and only 1 teaspoon warm water at step 2. This can be cooked in a greased 600ml (1pt) Pyrex measuring jug as for basic recipe.
Apple sponge pudding: grease but do not base-line the 900ml (1½pt) basin. Place 1 good heaped tablespoon of stewed apples in the bottom of the basin and spread mixture on top. Microwave on HIGH for 4 min. Alternatively, use other stewed fruit, such as rhubarb, gooseberries etc.
Jam/Marmalade/Syrup sponge pudding: proceed as for apple sponge, using 2 tablespoons jam, marmalade or golden syrup instead of apples. Cook on HIGH for 3½ min.

Seven day menus

Note: Mid-day and evening meals are interchangeable to suit lifestyle.

Sunday

BRUNCH
Browning Dish Brunch
toast, butter and marmalade

EVENING MEAL
chilled melon
Seasoned Chicken Joint
jacket or boiled new potatoes
Three-minute Buttered Carrots
brussels sprouts
cheese, biscuits, celery

Monday

BREAKFAST
fruit juice
muesli

SNACK LUNCH
Main Course Frankfurter and Bean Soup
crusty or wholemeal bread or bread roll
fresh fruit in season

EVENING MEAL
Minced Beef
mashed potatoes
vegetables (in season or frozen)
Chocolate Nutty Pears

Tuesday

BREAKFAST
Breakfast Grapefruit
wholemeal rolls with honey

SNACK LUNCH
Pitta Steaklet
fruit yoghurt

EVENING MEAL
Vegetarian Casserole
Baked Stuffed Apple

Wednesday

BREAKFAST
Breakfast kippers

SNACK LUNCH
Burger with salad

EVENING MEAL
Ham and Mushroom Risotto
Quick Fruit Crumble

Thursday

BREAKFAST
fruit juice
Porridge

SNACK LUNCH
Pie and Mushy Peas
fresh fruit in season

EVENING MEAL
Store-cupboard Crispy Tuna
sweetcorn or broad beans
Fruited Sponge Pudding

Friday

BREAKFAST
Compôte of Dried Fruit

SNACK LUNCH
soup in a cup
Muffin Rarebit

EVENING MEAL
Convenient Fish 'n' Chips
Baked Egg Custard

Saturday

BREAKFAST
Warm croissants
fresh fruit in season

SNACK LUNCH
Macaroni with Cheese and Ham

EVENING MEAL
Spicy Spare Ribs
Boiled Long-grain Rice
Raspberry Delight

Microwave short cuts

Skinning a fresh peach is easier if it is first heated on HIGH for 15–30 sec.

Citrus fruits will yield more juice after heating for only 30 sec on HIGH.

Currants, raisins or sultanas which have shrivelled after long storage can be easily plumped. Place them in a bowl with just enough water to cover. Cover the bowl and microwave on HIGH for 3 min. Stir and leave to stand, covered, for 5 min.

Freshen a stale bread roll or bun by heating for 10 sec. Serve warm.

Ice-cream is easier to scoop if heated for a few seconds.

Brie and Camembert cheese can be ripened using LOW setting. Allow 15–30 sec for 75g (3oz) and stand for a few minutes before serving.

Reheat leftover cold coffee on HIGH, allowing 1½ min per cup.

Don't waste small amounts of jam left in the bottom of jars. Remove metal lid from jar, place in oven and heat on HIGH for 10–20 sec, depending on quantity.

Packet jellies are quickly prepared. Place the cut-up cubes in an ovenproof bowl with 150ml (¼pt) water. Microwave on HIGH for 1½ min or until cubes have melted, checking and stirring after 1 min. Make up to required amount with cold water and/or ice cubes.

Dissolve gelatine in seconds. For example, 15g (½oz) gelatine in 3 tablespoons water takes only 15–30 sec on HIGH. Stir until completely dissolved.

Melt 100g (4oz) chocolate in a bowl in 1½ min. Stir after 1 min and do not overheat.

To skin tomatoes, pierce skins and place in boiling water. Microwave on HIGH for 30 sec. Plunge into a bowl of cold water and remove skins.

Soften hardened brown sugar by placing a wedge of apple with 100g (4oz) brown sugar in a dish. Cover and heat on HIGH for 15–30 sec. Check after 15 sec and if sugar has started to soften, remove it from the oven and leave to stand 5 min. Do not overheat. Remove from the oven if the sugar starts to melt.

Seasoned chicken joint (page 32); Three minute buttered carrots (:page 36); Brussels sprouts (page 40); Boiled new potatoes (page 40) – on Adams Sharon

Guide to defrosting some everyday and convenience foods

Food	Quantity	Approximate Time on LOW Setting	Special Instructions
Bread			
loaf	1 small	4–6 min	Wrap in kitchen paper; turn over during defrosting; stand 10 min
pitta	2	1½–2 min	Place on kitchen paper; turn over during defrosting
slice	1×25g (1oz)	10–15 sec	Place on kitchen paper
rolls	2	45–60 sec	Place on kitchen paper; stand 2–3 min
croissant	2	30–60 sec	Place on kitchen paper; stand for 2 min. Warning: outside will be soft
currant buns	2	45–60 sec	Place on kitchen paper; stand 3 min
Cakes			
dairy cream doughnut	1	30 sec	Remove from package; place on kitchen paper; stand 5 min
dairy cream éclairs	2	30–45 sec	Remove from package; place on kitchen paper; stand 10 min
dairy cream sponge	1×6 portion	1½ min	Remove from package; place on kitchen paper; stand 20–25 min
fruit topped cheesecake	1×6 portion	4 min	Remove from foil tray; place on kitchen paper; stand 20–30 min
jam doughnut	1	1½ min	Place on kitchen paper; stand 2 min
mince pies, cooked	2	30–45 sec	Place on kitchen paper; stand 5 min; time depends on size
small cakes, buns	2	1–1½ min	Place on kitchen paper or microwave roasting rack; stand 5 min; time depends on size
Fish			
fillets, cutlets, steaks	225g (½lb)	3–4 min	Cover, and separate during defrosting
whole fish	450g (1lb)	6–8 min	Cover; turn over during defrosting; stand 5–10 mins
rainbow trout	1×175g (7oz)	3½ min	Slit pack and place on a plate; stand 5 min
prawns	225g (8oz)	3–4 min	Slit pouch; flex during defrosting; stand 5 min
kipper, whole or fillets	225g (8oz)	3 min	Cover; separate fillets during defrosting; stand 5 min

Meat and Poultry

bacon rashers	225g (8oz)	2–3 min	Turn pack over during defrosting; stand 5 min
braising steak, cubed	225g (8oz)	4–5 min	Cover; rearrange during defrosting; stand 5 min; use immediately
chops	2 × 100g (4oz)	4–5 min	Separate during defrosting; stand 5 min
liver, kidney	225g (8oz)	4–5 min	Separate during defrosting; stand 5 min; use immediately
minced beef	225g (8oz)	4–5 min	Cover; break up during defrosting; stand 5 min; use immediately
sausages	225g (8oz)	3–4 min	Separate during defrosting; stand 5 min; use immediately
Chicken drumsticks	2 × 100g (4oz)	4–5 min	Turn over during defrosting; stand 5 min
portions	2 × 225g (8oz)	7–9 min	Turn over during defrosting; stand 10 min

Miscellaneous

butter or margarine	250g (8.82oz) pack	$1\frac{1}{2}$–$1\frac{3}{4}$ min	Remove from wrapper; place on a plate; turn over during defrosting; stand 5 min
fruit juice concentrate	178ml ($6\frac{1}{4}$oz)	3 min	Remove collar and lid before defrosting; dilute with cold water
mousse	1 individual	30 sec	Remove lid; stand 15–20 min
pastry	1 × 212g ($7\frac{1}{2}$oz) pack	1 min	Defrost in pack; stand 20–30 min
pâté	1 × 198g (7oz) pack	3–4 min	Unwrap and place on plate; cover; stand at least 15 min
trifle or melba	1 individual	1 min	Remove lid; stand 15–20 min
yoghurt	1 × 125g (4.4oz) carton	3 min	Remove lid; stir for 1 min after defrosting to mix

Guide to reheating non-frozen cooked and canned foods

Food	Quantity or Weight	Approximate Time on HIGH Setting	Special Instructions
baked beans (canned)	150g (5.3oz) 219g ($7\frac{3}{4}$oz)	50–60 sec 1–$1\frac{1}{2}$ min	Turn into covered bowl; stir once during heating
beef, sliced with gravy	1 serving	1–2 min	Place on covered non-metallic plate or dish
casserole or stew	1 serving 2 servings	2–3 min 4–5 min	Cover and stir during heating
chicken portions	1 × 225g (8oz) 2 × 225g (8oz)	$1\frac{1}{2}$–2 min 3–4 min	Cover and turn over during heating
Fruit pie	1 portion	30 sec	Place on non-metallic serving plate

Christmas pudding	1 portion 2 portions	30–45 sec 45 sec–1¼ min	Place in serving dish; cover with plastic wrap; stand 1 min; DO NOT OVERHEAT; actual time will depend on size of portions
Cornish pasty	1	45 sec–1¼ min	Place on kitchen paper; stand 2 min; time depends on size
garden peas (canned)	284g (10oz)	2–2½ min	Turn into covered bowl; stir during heating
Macaroni cheese (canned)	210g (7.4oz)	1¼–½ min	Turn into covered bowl; stir during heating
Meat pie	1 individual	45 sec–1¼ min	Remove from foil container; place on microwave roasting rack or kitchen paper; stand 2–3 min
milk pudding (canned)	435g (15½oz)	2½–3 min	Turn into covered bowl; stir during heating
mince pies	1 4	5–10 sec 20–30 sec	Place on kitchen paper or microwave roasting rack; DO NOT OVERHEAT; stand 2 min
pizza	1×10cm (4in)	2 min	Place on kitchen paper or microwave roasting rack; DO NOT OVERHEAT; stand 2 min
pre-plated main course	1	2–3 min	Cover with plastic wrap; rotate if necessary during heating
quiche	1 portion	45–60 sec	Place on kitchen paper; stand 2 min; time depends on size
rice, long grain (refrigerated)	1 serving 2 servings	1¼–1½ min 2–2½ min	Place with 2 teaspoons water in covered casserole; stir during heating
soup	1 serving	2½–3 min	Turn into covered soup bowl; stir during heating
spaghetti in tomato sauce (canned)	213g (7½oz)	1½–2½ min	Turn into covered bowl; stir during heating
tomatoes (canned)	227g (8oz)	1½–2 min	Turn into covered bowl; stir during heating
vegetables (cooked)	225g (8oz) 450g (1lb)	2 min 3–4 min	Place in covered bowl with 2 tablespoons water; stir during heating

Index

Numbers in **bold** refer to illustrations

First published 1987
Reprinted 1994
Reprinted 1997

Photography: Stan Weale

Typesetting:
Ace Filmsetting, Frome

Colour separations:
Gilchrist Brothers, Leeds

Printed by Graphycems for
Angell Editions
39 Coombeshead Road
Newton Abbot, Devon

British Library Cataloguing in Publication Data

Weale, Margaret
  Microwave recipes for one or two.
  1. Microwave cookery.
  I. Title
  641.5′882   TX832

ISBN 0 948432 50 0